The
Draconic
Code
Daily

UNICURSAL

M~A RICARD

The Draconic Code

Daily

DRACONIA BOOK 2

UNICURSAL

TABLE OF CONTENT

THE DRACONIC CODE DAILY

THE ELEVEN DRACONIC SEALS

The Science of Dragons

THE Science of Dragons is the science of life. Draconic Science is the science of the occult, of Magick, of energies, of good, balance and light. Choosing to work with dragons means wanting to specialize in a magickal path, without however denying the others. It is choosing to work closely with the Draconic Beings with complete awareness, love and, of course, affinity.

Dragons, like many other universal creatures, are very happy to obtain this recognition and love that we carry for them. Their maturity not being equal, just like for men, there will always be these dragons with a more mischievous temperament who will greatly enjoy getting this attention, while the wiser ones will be more reserved, discreet and less eager to show their contentment, a bit like a grandfather with an unchanging phlegm who, with a smirk, looks affectionately at his more turbulent grandchildren. That being said, all however appreciate being recognized and express some joy in receiving these thoughts carrying beneficial messages about them. But even more, they rejoice when the conscious Being finally manages to tune into their vibrational frequency, and communicates with them, humbly asking them for assistance to perform good deeds with their precious help.

As an eclectic magician who learned the trade and his Art in a self-taught and solitary way, like the majority (if not all) of us, never would I have thought possible, fifteen years ago, that by writing a book about Dragon Magick, this topic would become so popular... and how much even more to this day. But moreover, through the many letters, comments, emails and so on, how the Science of dragons was not only booming, but that a growing, even exponential, number of daraco[1] followers, occultism and dragon enthusiasts already existed in anonymity, and that dragons would take such a privileged place in Magick.

---

1   *Daraco*, as put forth in the first book, *Draconia*, is the name given to designate the draconic magician.

Ironically, when I started to write what would eventually become *Draconia*, somewhere around May 2002, I simply had in mind to write a book for my own personal pleasure, nothing more. I had always dreamed of finding a book on Magick and dragons, but, alas, there was nothing satisfying that existed on this topic. It was either one or the other, or just fantasy books and nothing serious in the field of Ceremonial Magick. Since I had a lot of material in hand about dragons and because that coveted book on Draconic Magick didn't exist, I thought to myself, it looks like I'm the one who's going to have to write it! And so, in order to give myself a gift, I started to write the book that I had always wished I could find in bookstores. Some people asked me at that time if I thought the book would ever become popular or appreciated, if people would eventually want to read it and put it into practice. I remember then answering that it was just not important. I only needed to write it and put forth its knowledge for anyone who would ever want to enquire it. I often repeated that if this book came to please me, then, inevitably, it could do nothing else but to please someone else in return.

At first, I simply wanted to collect my own personal notes and gather my researches on Magick and dragons. I was far from realizing that sharing my knowledge and the fruit of these long hours of work with my faithful companions PNFYR and *Zeta* was going to make Draconic Magick my personal flagship. And so passed the days, nights, weeks, months and, finally, I arrived with the finished product that you know today: *Draconia, Draconic Teachings of True Dragon Magick.*

I still remember that sunny summer afternoon, when I was with my family in the company of an extraordinary woman who, as it were, was also a psychic. We were discussing about various things pertaining to the esoteric realm and it was then that the subject of familiars, these companions of the invisible, surfaced. I simply asked her what she perceived, without revealing anything to her. She very clearly saw my dear companion PNFYR and described him standing close behind me, wings outstretched. She saw him floating in the ether and even told me his name. I knew then that, indeed, it was my draconic friend. She then focused a little deeper in order to establish a better contact. What followed was rather unusual. He communicated to her how happy he was to be mentioned in a book. She then told me a little jokingly:

"You know, your dragon... he seems to really enjoy being in the spotlight. He says he loves being the star!"

There was a big laugh.

I had, once again, proof that dragons, just like other invisible Beings in the creation, can sometimes be blessed with a very good sense of humor! But what PNFYR really wanted to tell us, is that our dear dragons were happy to be recognized as living Beings and not as supernatural characters belonging to fairy tales. They simply are. That's it.

So, the question we can ask ourselves today would probably be this: Why did I wait so long, so many years later to write a new book on dragons?

Well, the answer is quite simple. Although you have asked me many times for a second volume, I simply could not write it before because science, any science that is, cannot be invented... it is discovered! I had therefore not yet found it, nor learned all these new techniques that I can, finally, share with you today. Indeed, I believe that it is never a good idea to write a book just to write a book! One needs to have new material, information and ideas to communicate with others. And since this is now the case, I am very happy to be able to share this new knowledge with you, these few additional pages about our fellow dragons and the Magickal Art.

For sure, dragons are still fascinating and it is not soon before this will likely come to change. And mostly for the draconic magician. For this individual, more than anyone, knows not only how to recognize the existence of dragons as Beings in their own right, living on a different plane from ours, but more as venerable friends of the Great Brotherhood and precious magician assistants.

For your infinite patience, I do thank you. I hope with all my heart that you will appreciate these new teachings of the Draconic Art. And before leaving you, I would like to thank all the readers, friends of the dragons, daracos and all of you for all your warm comments and the welcome you gave when the first book was released. May the Divine Providence stay close to you every step of the way. Keep up doing good, you do it so well.

Fraternally in Draconia,

M-A Ricard ~555

How to use this book

THIS draconic manual is divided into two distinct parts besides an appendix the reader will find at the very end. As such, there is no real way to put into practice the Draconic Code presented here, nor any chronological order to follow except that for each of the eleven Golden rules of the Code, we will find:

- its number,
- its statement,
- its explanation (*in italics*),
- followed by additional information,
- a magickal practice,
- as well as a Draconic Seal.

In the first part of the book, you will find each of the rules as well as its original description, followed by an even more detailed explanation demonstrating its use in a modern, mundane or magickal context. You will be able to better understand the Draconic Laws by these new comments, the which will open new vistas to explore. Then will follow its practical application, that is to say, the exercise which will put forward this rule of the Draconic Code into an everyday life context. In other words, how can you, the draconic magician, express this rule of conduct on a daily basis by taking concrete action, whether it is a ritual, a gesture, a meditation or an invocation. It is here that you will make Dragon Magick a renewed celebration, day after day, within a magickal way of life that will remain intimately yours.

Finally, all these considerations aside, you will find in the second part of the book a rather surprising and powerful new draconic practice, putting forth new tools available to the magician, namely the eleven *Draconic Seals*. These are glyphs of power representing the moving forces associated with the laws of the Draconic Code. You will have the opportunity to work with very special magickal Sigils that will act as energy accumulators in order to bring you closer, once again, to your dragon assistants.

You are free to follow these exercises in the order presented here or to leaf through this book and choose one of the rules of the Draconic Code that appeals to you the most at this moment in your life. It will happen that, for some reason, you do not know yet, that such and such a rule will seem to reach you more, even more deeply than another. If so, a careful study of the implications of this draconic statement is to be done. Read the law in question, then read it again, and a third time if necessary. Sometimes certain passages that are more obscure or more simplistic in appearance will reveal new information to you. If necessary, write everything down in your personal diary. Eventually, by re-reading your writings, you will come to discover in what circumstances you will have had new experiences in Draconia.

As it is never easy for an author to take for granted that the reader already knows the material contained in the previous works, the appendix available at the end of this book is intended as a modest supplement so that this manual is sufficient on its own to practice your Draconic Magick, without having to constantly refer you to the first book. You still have, as far as possible, a practical guide that can be used on its own without having read anything beforehand. Obviously, one will never go without the other and it is in this sense that the reading of the first book of Draconic Magick, *Draconia*, is however warmly recommended in regard of all the additional information at your disposal. If necessary, you can always borrow a copy from a friend or take a trip to the library.

That being said, I will allow myself this last remark before we move on to the practical part of this work. Please try not to spread yourself too thin. In this regard, you should never jump from one rule to another without, at the very least, having completed a cycle of five to seven days, as far as the use of Seals is concerned. One of the obvious reasons being that the time for an action to manifest will be shortened or, worse, will overlap a similar but not necessarily complementary force of action. It would be like a magician crafting several talismans for different needs and then deciding to wear them all at once, simultaneously. Not only would there be too great a mix of energies, vibrations, but even more, each subtle force would be weakened by its following. In short, pure and simple chaos.

This is why I recommend that you take all the time necessary to complete each occult action before moving on to the next one. Your results will be even more convincing, rest assured.

THE DRACONIC CODE DAILY

The Draconic Code Daily

FOR several years now, we have known this chivalric code of conduct intimately related to Dragon Magick. The latter was featured in my first book on Draconia. These are of course the eleven Golden rules constituting what is referred to as the Draconic Code. Being scrupulously followed by dragons, they obviously expect the daracos to do the same in return, because in the end, the Code expresses eminently well the qualities required for the conduct of draconic magicians in the perfection of their Art as well as their souls.

I have noticed over the years that besides its study and meaning so much truthful, many practical applications could also be drawn from it. Thus, it is true that in addition to following the way of the dragons and adhering to the Code, the magician who has captured this attraction for the Magickal Science will now be able to implement these laws by concrete actions, here now, and this, on every day of his life.

Care must be taken here about the way we use the word "law". When I say this or that law of the Draconic Code, it is a simple term which is intended to be interchangeable with Golden rule or rule of conduct, statements, etc. In truth, these are not mandatory laws in the proper sense of the term. Like, for example, to follow these and bow to them or give up Draconic Magick. Not at all. We couldn't be further from the truth. Rather, these so-called laws constituting the Draconic Code are seen as ideals, guidelines or, if you prefer, venerable advice to follow when we wish to take the path leading to a magickal life in Draconia. After all, you will always have the right to choose between understanding and applying or simply refusing and walk away, as indicated by the third statement: *Free Will and Freedom of Choice.*

That being clarified, for most draconic magicians, studying and understanding the Code should be, all in all, quite easy. This is rather reassuring. After several readings one will also find snippets of wisdom hidden here and there throughout the text. However, only an in-depth and meticulous study will reveal these splendors and only afterwards shall they be perceived and understood. Alright, but then what else? Wouldn't there be a way to make it a personal process, constantly renewed, in order to live Draconic Magick in a more intense way, in order to make it more vivid? Well yes, it is possible and that is exactly the aim of this book: to provide everyone with a practical developing structure in Draconic Magick that the daraco will be able to apply as often as he wishes, rain or shine, in his daily life.

This structure or, if you prefer, this *magickal and practical application of the Draconic Code,* is not strictly speaking a training in Draconic Magick either. Rather, it is an eminently practical amalgamation of exercises, rituals, meditations, and invocations designed and delivered by the dragons to make the daraco more sensitive to its magickal surroundings.

It is an undeniable fact that choosing the Draconic Path means getting involved and following a valuable teaching, to develop oneself magically, spiritually and working closely with our dragon assistants. Therefore, living its Art daily will not only make you a greater, stronger, more powerful draconic magician, but also and above all, closer than ever to dragon Beings and Entities.

When living by the Draconic Code, one cannot help but think of this popular adage which states that the game is well worth the candle. This is absolutely true; it is even a certainty. And know that the light glowing from this Draconic candle is simply... magnificent.

Deep Respect of Dragons

ℰℭ

Draconic Entities and all Draconia Beings are to be respected in all circumstances, as well as for the works they perform, whether visibly or invisibly, on this plane of existence or another, in this life or in another. Dragons are Beings of rare erudition. Their advice demonstrates great and profound wisdom. They are allies of the daraco and you must treat them as your equals.

D RAGONS are very powerful Entities and they
rejoice when they have the opportunity to
help their fellow magicians during their esoteric, magickal and spiritual workings. It goes without saying that having respect for dragons is para-
mount in Draconia if one wants, for all practical
purposes, obtain some kind of results. This respect
is not only meant at the level of language and ex-
pression, particularly about how to express yourself
when you want to address them, but also on the level
of thoughts and actions taken throughout your daily
life. A magician is no less responsible once his ceremonial clothes have been removed and that he has
left his magickal sanctuary.

In order to properly manifest this first law or
Golden rule, the daraco will regularly give the dragons a sacrifice in order to honor them, to recognize
them in their work and, of course, so as to forge an
ever closer bound with them.

Fortunately, the sacrifice of which I speak here
has nothing to do with the barbaric rite of killing an

animal. It is true, as it was earlier mentioned about them[2], dragons will ask some kind of payment in return for services rendered, yes, but never in terms of material offerings or bloody sacrifices. They want to see you improve and grow. Thus, this sacrificial act, even if it remains optional, will be done by an exchange of energy occurring on a psychic level; a wave of light and compassion towards them, drawn from your own vital force, in order to show them your love, your gratitude and your allegiance.

Not only will you be helping the dragons in their daily energy workings, by providing them support on the emotional plane, but moreover, you will also be acting as their flagbearer, so to speak, on the material plane, which for them will be a real blessing.

The Dragon Sacrifice

Set up your altar table with one of your candlesticks, incense burner and Draconic Pentacle. Light a white candle and burn some good quality incense.

---

2 *Draconia*, p.57, The First Steps: Questing for Dragons.

You can use dragon's blood or frankincense, rose or sage. If desired, and this is what I recommend you to do, practice the Draconic Cross ritual[3] in order to purify and clean your workplace on the psychic level.

Then, take place in the center of your sanctuary facing East. Stand or sit on the ground, close your eyes and center yourself. Empty your mind and tap into the Source. Stay in a passive state of mind for a short moment and meditate in silence.

When you'll feel time is right, that you are convinced to be in communion with the hosts of Draconia, formulate mentally or verbally your call to the dragons in words such as:

I call here in this place,
The presence of the Dragons,
Of all planes,
Of all Elements,
Of all races,
And of all Spheres.
Come to me,
I, the Daraco who summons you.
Come, haste and listen.

---

3   See appendix for the complete procedure.

In the silence of the heart, be aware of your surroundings. Listen passively and stay alert. Take note of any visions, impressions or emotions you may be experiencing. In a short time, you could become aware of a presence, or even several, close to you.

Now, place your right hand on your Draconic Pentacle and raise your left hand, palm forward, elbow at about 90 degrees, much the same way you would if you were to solemnly swear on a bible.

Take a deep breath and focus again. You are at the center of a great Draconic assembly. You have called forth Entities and they have answered. Visualize as clearly as possible any nearby dragons in front of you waiting for your call to follow. They have introduced themselves to you and are patiently awaiting in silence and respect the course of your upcoming actions. Then pronounce, mentally or verbally:

On this Pentacle which is the support
of Elemental Forces,
Dragon from here and there,
I offer you this pledge in good faith.

Visualize a flame shooting out of the palm of your left hand and radiating out in front of you in a 180 degrees arc, like the beam of a powerful flashlight. This light of a golden white is intense and extremely bright. It radiates an unparallelled warmth and fills the room with a soothing aura. The more you breathe in, the more each following exhalation will nourish in return this light, which is in fact your own vital force, that you consciously diffuse towards the Entities present in your sanctuary.

See the dragons in front of you. They remain impassive as ever and express uncommon righteousness and wisdom. Watch them receive your sacrifice and rejoice in it. It is as if you projected a beam of light onto each of them which allowed them to charge their batteries and commune with you.

After a short while[4], it will be time to stop projecting your sacrifice. Clench the fist of the left hand and immediately, see the light which was projected from it extinguish right away.

____

4   Pay attention. Although this technique does not include any risk for the operator, the latter still relieves himself of his own vital force, the which is given to feed Entities. Even though this method may seem questionable to some, it remains harmless as long as the energy released remains controlled. In fact, it could easily sound like, by analogy, a person donating blood for a blood bank.

Still holding your position, fist raised and right hand on the Pentacle, conclude this dedicatory act and thank the Draconic Beings for having answered to your call, in similar words:

Dragons of all planes,
Of all Elements,
Of all races,
And of all Spheres.
I have offered you this pledge in good faith,
May you use it for the Great Work.
I, the Daraco who called you forth,
I thank you for your presence.
Leave now and find your own Spheres,
Peace be forever between you and us.
Draconis, draconis, draconis.

Give the Triple Sign [5].

Visualize the image of the dragons quietly fading away until you can no longer see them. They have now left your sanctuary. You are alone once more in the quietness of your magickal temple. Calmly return

---

5   See appendix for the complete procedure.

to your normal state of consciousness and practice the Draconic Cross one last time, in order to dissipate wandering energies and any Astral Entities that may have been attracted as a result of this sacrifice. Extinguish the candle between your thumb and forefinger. The rite is completed.

 **II**

Respect for Universal Creatures

ೞ

The daraco recognizes that he is not the master of the Earth, but rather that he coexists in harmony with all Universal creatures. From dragons to men, from animals to trees, from plants to stones; all play a significant role within the balance of the One. Every action, big or small, affects another, and we are all connected to each other. Size, look and shape don't matter; all living creatures have their unique purpose.

THIS law from the Draconic Code can be expressed in many different ways. By taking this statement literally, we obviously guess that respecting one's neighbor, regardless of his reign, whether it be human, animal, vegetable or mineral, knowing how to remain close to existential nature is essential. In this perspective, outdoor and nature enthusiasts will understand more than anyone else how important it is to respect this Golden rule. Someone who knows how to live in harmony with his surroundings, the fauna and flora, knowing how to behave in society, taking care of himself and others as well as respecting the environment is an asset for Mother Earth.

You can therefore spend a few moments every day for this purpose in order to become aware of the life around you. Go outside and look around everywhere. Feel the air caressing your face. Hear the chirping of birds, the noise from automobiles, the laughter of children playing in the distance. Look at your feet and the ground below. You are on the

Earth, this same Earth which supports nature, grass, wheat, trees, houses; Earth which supports stones and mountains, lakes and rivers; which provides food for men as well as animals and insects...

Meditate on how a simple action you take today will eventually affect your environment, your neighbour. Try to determine for a short moment what place you occupy, at this moment, in this vast Universe. Try to figure out why size, look and shape don't matter. Recognize that in this world, everything is relative; what seems small or very large to you may seem very large or very small to another. Be aware that if you were as tiny as an ant, how different things would look to you, and yet remains the same, since only their proportions would be changed. It is then that you will understand even better the bond that unite you to each other and why all living creatures have their reason for being.

Now, if we pay attention to a more occult and magickal side of this same draconic statement, we also understand by *"all universal creatures"*, therefore, all creation, that all that exists and surrounds us, which moves, lives and dies, is in fact due to the action of the Elements. We are not always aware of it, nor do we see how these elemental forces act and collide, but the fact remains that everything is credited to them. This elemental action which is called Astral Light or terrestrial fluid is also designated as the Great Magnetic Agent, the Od, or more commonly in occultism, by the electromagnetic fluid. On the other hand, if we extrapolate a little further, we can also add that the empire of the will over the Astral Light, which is so to speak, the physical soul of the four Elements, is represented in Magick by the symbol of the Pentagram, of which the upper point (surmounted by the fifth Element Spirit or Akâsha), is oriented upwards.

By taking the time to properly understand this latest information, we can then affirm without fear of being mistaken that "all *universal creatures*" stands for "*all elemental forces at work.*"

You should too know that the human body is also governed by the action of these same Elements. Let's not forget, our body, the microcosm (or small Universe) is modeled after the macrocosm, the large Universe. Also, the seat of the head is ruled by Fire. The torso is subject to the influences of the Air Element. The region of the lower abdomen is under the action of Water, and finally, the rest of the lower body, under the Earth Element. In the same way, the elemental action also affects human temperaments and behaviours.

When we then study all the associations pertaining to the Cosmic Elements and apply these patterns in a Ceremonial Magick context, we obtain for these four forces, or fundamental essences, different analogical tables. In particular, the associations found on the next page (Table 1).

As we can see, the Cosmic Elements, being the basis of everything, namely Fire, Water, Air and Earth, are the four primordial pillars on which the Universe rests. It is therefore not surprising to understand why the daraco will regularly invoke these elemental forces during his rites in order to awaken the powers of nature and cosmos. Through these acts of invocation, it will be possible for him to get in tune with these same natural forces in order to harmonize his own structure, physical, astral and mental, in a balance essential to magickal and draconic practices.

We find next (Fig.1) the four pairs of Pentagrams that we know and that we already use in our rites in order to invoke and banish elemental forces. The following Invocation to the Dragons of the Elements will make no exception of this rule and thus, will use the same Pentagrams.

Fire	Water	Air	Earth
△	▽	◬	⍖
Spiritual	Astral	Mental	Physical
South	West	East	North
Red	Blue	Yellow	Green/Black
Ram Lion Sagittarius	Cancer Scorpio Pisces	Gemini Balance Aquarius	Taurus Virgo Capricorn
Yod	He	Vau	He
Atziluth/ Archetype	Briah/ Creation	Yetzirah/ Formation	Assiah/ Manifestation
Lion	Eagle	Man	Bull
Head	Lower- abdomen	Torso	Legs
Wand	Cup	Dagger	Pentacle
Salamanders	Undines	Sylphs	Gnomes
Michael	Gabriel	Raphael	Oriel
Fafnyr	Naëlyan	Sairys	Graël
Dragons of Magma & Volcanoes	Dragons of the Seas & Aquatic Bodies	Dragons of Winds & Storms	Dragons of Forests & Mountains

Table 1.
Some Elemental correspondences

Before going any further, take a short break and reread, if necessary, what has just been said in order to fully understand these slightly more complex explanations. Know that for a magician, doing something knowing that it will result in something else is never enough. Just like a scientist who studies the genetic code with the aim of duplicating it, the practitioner of the Art must understand how the forces he manipulates work and interact in order to be able to manifest them and use them wisely, each time.

Daily Invocation to Dragons of the Elements

Perform the Draconic Cross. Then move clockwise around your magic circle, which was just traced by the practice of the previous Major Rite, to the East. Trace the Invoking Pentagram of Air using your dagger of the same Element (in the event that you have your Draconic Magick tools) or using your index finger, visualizing it in a bright and pulsating yellow. Take a deep breath, then point the blade (or index finger) at the center of the Pentagram while vibrating:

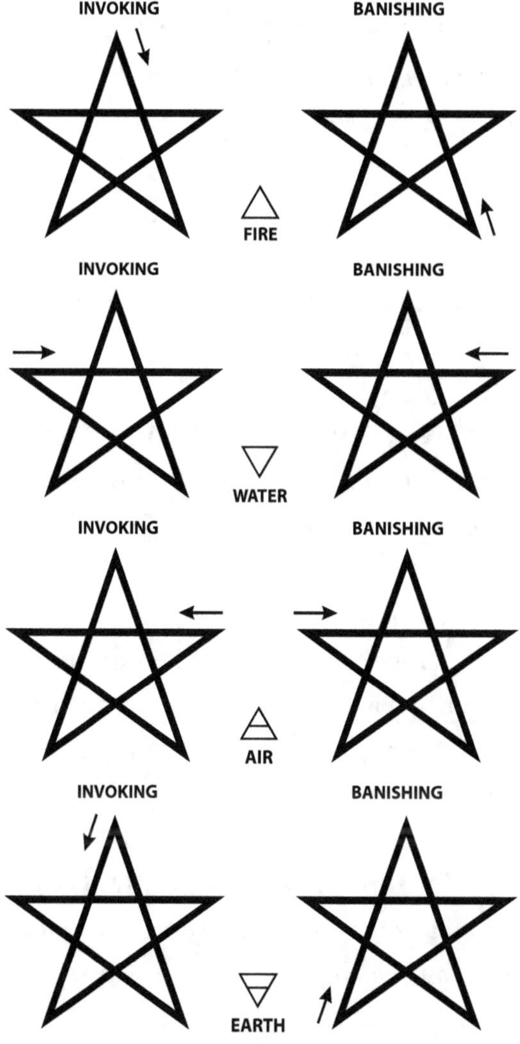

Figure 1.
Invoking & Banishing Pentagrams

OL VAVIN ILS MICALZO VOVIN EXARP

(Oel Vavini Ilâsâ Mikalazodo Vovini Etzarpeh)
"I call upon you mighty Dragons of the Air."

Head South. Trace the Invoking Pentagram of Fire using your wand (or index finger). Visualize this Pentagram of a very bright fiery red. Then point the wand at the center and vibrate:

OL VAVIN ILS MICALZO VOVIN BITOM

(Oel Vavini Ilâsâ Mikalazodo Vovini Bitomeh)
"I call upon you mighty Dragons of Fire."

Then circumambulate to the edge of the circle, to the West. Trace the Invoking Pentagram of Water with your cup, visualizing it in a sparkling electric blue. Point the cup in the center of the Pentagram and vibrate:

OL VAVIN ILS MICALZO VOVIN HCOMA

(Oel Vavini Ilâsâ Mikalazodo Vovini Hecomah)
"I call upon you mighty Dragons of Water."

Finally complete your circle and head North. Trace the Invoking Pentagram of the Earth using the pentacle, visualizing it electric green. Then point to the center of the Pentagram and vibrate:

OL VAVIN ILS MICALZO VOVIN NANTA
(Oel Vavini Ilâsâ Mikalazodo Vovini Naentah)
"I call upon you mighty Dragons of the Earth."

Return to your original position facing East. Take some time to visualize and contemplate the elemental Invoking Pentagrams that circles you and shine brightly with incredible vividness. After a short period of time meditating on the invoked energy, recite:

DOOAIN TOFGLO OD TOLTORG,
OL VAVIN ILS
(Do-ò-a-inu Tofajilo Od Toltoreji, Oel Vavini Ilâsâ)
"In the name of all things and creatures, I invoke you."

You can at this point accomplish two things at once, perform any type of second-rate occult or draconic work at your leisure, or simply close your eyes, relax and let yourself be bathed in this powerful elemental energy that has been stirred in your sanctuary.

If you applied yourself properly while performing this ritual of calling dragons of the Elements, you should, in a short time, feel energized, even overexcited as if you had drunk several cups of strong coffee. If this should happen, and inevitably it will, don't be afraid. Instead, just welcome this new sensation calmly and let it flow throughout your body.

When you'll decide it's time to put an end to this invigorating practice, trace, one by one, the Banishing Pentagrams facing each of the respective Watchtowers. Perform this in the same order as you did for invoking, that is to say starting at the East, then to the South, West and finally North. Conclude by performing once again the Draconic Cross in order to banish and return all wandering energies back to the realms where they belong.

III

Free Will and Freedom of Choice

ೞ

We all have free will, and that freedom allows us to choose what feels right and appropriate to us, even if later those choices turn out to be wrong or negative. Choosing means it is possible to make mistakes, and through these, great life lessons can be learned. Draconia is a science and a way of life working along Universal Energies, but it should not be seen as the only path to follow, nor will it be presented as such. Several paths lead to the top of a mountain and everyone has the right to take their own trail with regard to opinions, beliefs, religions or codes of conduct.

THIS statement tells us several things. In particular, that life is sometimes a winding journey and that along the way, we will inevitably have to stop to make choices, and that through these, important life lessons will be lived and, we hope, retained and learned. This Golden rule also makes us understand that it is possible, when applied in a magickal context, to work with invisible forces and currents in order to shape them according to our needs of the moment, whichever they may be, to satisfy our will. We will also agree that to satisfy these same desires, we can come to make bad choices by following a biased reasoning, to think that such and such a thing will be good for us and that by performing Magick, we will come to fulfill these deficiencies to greatly enhance our daily lives. The learned daraco understands that he should always keep the good habit to question himself, to introspect, and of course to evaluate the pros and cons before moving on to the practical part of his Art if he wishes to acquire material, emotional or spiritual gains.

In some ways, at least for what is of our concern here in this matter, this law shouldn't come across as a revelation. Because frankly, every magician, witch and practitioner of the Magickal Arts should already be aware of the Law of Return and Attraction. We also fully understand this notion of making decisions, and that by these, consequences will result. Sometimes good, sometimes unpleasant, but all in all, life is a long road that we simply cannot follow without questioning ourselves and taking action. For to do so is to numb yourself and allow your magician's will to atrophy. It's losing your power, in a way. For a practitioner of Draconia, *it is better to choose and perish than to remain idle and suffer.*

Thus, the free will that is so intimately linked to the Law of Return is also known as Karma. But here, there, and now in Dragon Magick, free will and Karma, how does this all fit together? Well, in order to properly understand and interpret this law of Karma within this draconic law (Isn't it wonderful? one law within another law...) and to ensure that you can become aware of its impact in your everyday life, both mundane and during your magickal practices, some explanations are necessary.

I will sum up here my remarks as presented in my book on High Witchcraft: *White Magick*[6]. Since this applies exactly the same way for all practitioners of the Art, both the witch who lives Wicca than the follower of Draconia, I will make you profit from what has already been said, adapting my words as needed for Dragon Magick.

Everyone has heard of Karma at least once, for good or bad reasons. But what is it exactly? To begin with, Karma is a Universal law intimately linked to the cycles of incarnations. To properly accept this concept of life, know that you must believe in reincarnation and renewed cycles of life. Otherwise, the law of triple return will have no visible impact or effect on your consciousness, but of course you will still be subject to it, without realizing it. Remember, *being unaware of the existence of a law doesn't mean it will not be effective.*

One could think of Karma as a law of cause and effect. There is a cosmic matrix which preserves the memory of our lives and which records our actions and gestures, thoughts, words; in short, all our be-

---

6   *White Magick: High Witchcraft Complete Formulary,* Unicursal 2017.

haviors. Each action carried out is therefore recorded there. We call this the *Akashic Records*. This explains how it is possible for some trained magician and psychics to consult these archives of the past and also those still in an embryonic state. In a pictorial way, it would look like a library where everything remains inscribed and catalogued, past, present and future.

Karma serves primarily for the spiritual evolution of each individual. The primary goal of every human being should ideally be to get closer to perfection, learn from past mistakes so as not to commit them again in the future and finally pursue their path of spiritual evolution consciously in order to move on to a higher level of existence.

I also mentioned that everything will have to be paid back, *one day or another, in this life or in another.* This is one of the reasons why Karma can also be considered as a law of cause and effect. The experiences and the sufferings that you endure in this present life are also due to your Karma. The bad choices you have made as well as those actions of your past bring you, today, ordeals where you will once again be faced with the same choices. If you cannot overcome them and therefore, at the same time, purify your Karma, you will once again have to come back in a future incarnation in order to have once again the possibility of making the right choice when the time comes.

That being said, your Karma can therefore become heavier by accumulating karmic debts or can become lighter, little by little, depending on the choices you make throughout your life. It is up to you and you alone to make the choices that are necessary for your own good, not only as a practitioner of the Magickal Arts, but also as a being of spiritual nature. The secret to bypass Karma is yet so simple; always have a healthy life, direct your draconic practices towards noble goals and you will pretty much have nothing to worry about.

Consequently, the law of Karma, also known as the law of Triple Return, stipulates that what you bring into this life will affect your daily life by three times, and what you will experience will be in perfect analogy with your own actions and thoughts. In other words, give in to black magick and you'll be in trouble three times over. On the other hand, do good during your white magick rituals and you will create good around you threefold.

I agree, if you are thinking at this moment how easy it is to complicate your life with so many considerations, with occult laws, and how much the principle of free will *"it's my life, therefore it's my choice"*, can take on such magnitude when we begin to dissect this world of energies that surrounds us, to that I will that you are absolutely right. We must not become paranoid and start studying everything about each of our daily actions through endless divinations. True, sometimes it's better to just try, stumble and get back up. Simply take the time to think about the possible outcomes of your magickal practices before bringing them into action, so you can see if what you wish to obtain is truly a necessity and not just out of a personal fancy. Balance things out and trust your judgment. Everything will be fine, I'm sure.

*
**

Morning Introspection

The practical aspect of this third draconic statement is made of two parts. First, take a moment in the morning, a few minutes at most, soon after you wake up and meditate on what has just been said. Ponder on how the choices you made in the past have come to shape your tomorrows. Think about your draconic journey so far and ask yourself what you could improve today, this week or this month, to perfect your magickal training and how you could become an even more sensitive magician to the outside world, the invisible planes and to advices whispered by your fellow dragons, etc.

See in what circumstances, arising from your own actions or personal choices you have made, have led you so far. Was there a decision in your magickal life that you made in the past that backfired at you so that you can now deduce that it was the fruit of the Law of Return? On the contrary, do you lack the motivation to take action and dare to act? Let your thoughts flow in this direction and then determine what you think would work best for you in a close future and record your thoughts in your magickal diary. Later during the day or week, you will practice the following Draconic charge exercise to improve your current situation.

*
**

A Draconic Charge

The third rule of the Draconic Code tells us that in addition to the law of cause and effect, or rather, should I say, karmic decisions, actions and retributions, that you as a daraco, have the choice to choose what seems to be the best for you and opt to strive to obtain it. If you go in this direction, it is that you have decided to do like this witch who once said to me: "*If it seems good for you, then it must be good.*" In other words, do what feels right to you in the best of your judgment and if you feel comfortable with your choices, then that can only be good for you. Moreover, you also have the magickal wisdom, knowledge and all the tools required to awaken, attract and sublimate external influences so they can manifest themselves in your daily life on the plane of Malkuth[7].

As you should now be doing your morning introspection and that your immediate desire has been well thought and pointed out, you can then take action to manifest this wish in your daily life. There are many ways to achieve this, and one of them is through the surprising effects of a technique known in Draconia as the *Draconic charge*. That is to say, you will create

---

7 Malkuth, which means Kingdom in Hebrew, is the 10th Sephira of the Kabbalistic Tree of Life. It is associated with the four Elements $\triangle \triangledown \triangle \triangledown$ and the physical plane of matter. It corresponds to the same Sephira, ONDOH (in Enochian) that the daraco points to when practicing the Draconic Cross.

a kind of magic volt, a powerful transmitter whose material support will be a very special Draconic Sigil which will then be charged with the Draconic Force.

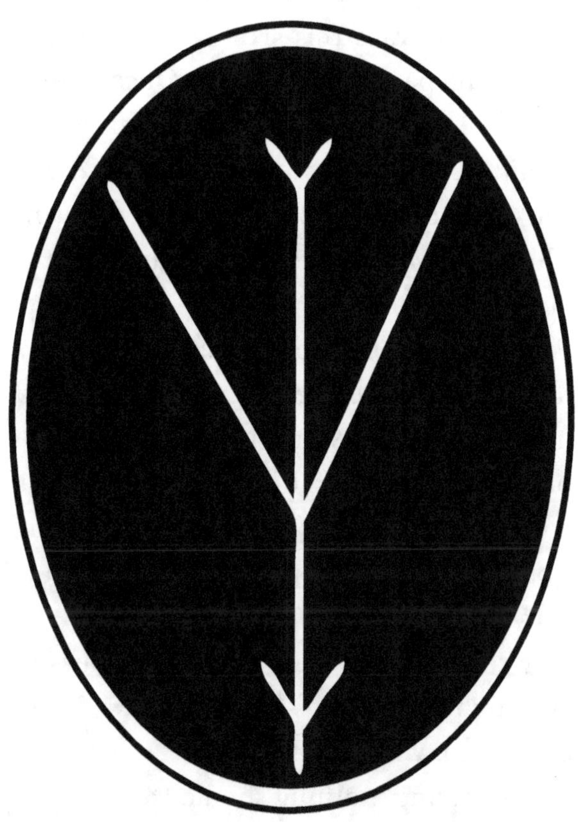

Figure 2.
Sigil for Draconic Charge

Once created according to the rules of the Art, this instrument will exalt the vibrations corresponding to the nature of the Force concerned, whether it be elemental, planetary, draconic or other.

To do this, you will use the figure as shown (Fig.2). You will trace this symbol in black ink on a piece of white parchment paper. Once completed, you will place it on your Draconic Pentacle (not the Earth Pentacle) in the center of your altar. Following this, you will build up the Draconic Force and use the technique of *direct induction* to infuse your charge with the desired faculty.

Take a comfortable position and relax. Visualize that you are at the center of the Universe and that in front of you is a beautiful sparkling and pulsating golden red sphere. This sphere is the Draconic Force. When you are able to picture it clearly in your mind, breathe in this energy deeply through all the pores of your skin.

Every time you inhale, your body draws in and stores this light which transfers from the sphere within you, through your whole body.

When exhaling, nothing should come out of your body. The Draconic Force will remain within you. Continue to accumulate this light by charging it with a specific quality (the one you should have chosen during your recent morning introspections) seeing it penetrate you from everywhere, until you feel that this energy is compressed to a maximum, like a balloon ready to burst. At this point, know that you have accumulated enough Draconic Force to use it for magickal purposes.

Place your hands above your magickal symbol. Now transfer the light-charge on the latter. This will pass through your hands to take place over the entire surface of the parchment. With each exhalation, visualize the light leaving your hands to attach itself to the object. See your Draconic charge glow brighter and brighter as it receives the light. Use as many exhalations to transfer the Draconic Force as there were inspirations to accumulate it in you. You will use this symbol as a talismanic image of your desire brought into manifestation. Your Draconic charge will work like a battery emitting a vibrational field that will transfer to your aura. You will carry it on your person for as long as you wish to manifest the acquisition of this quality. If you wish to use your magic charge for an extended period of time, then it would be recommended to repeat the whole charging process at regular intervals, such as once a month for example, so that it can maintain its effectiveness. When it is no longer needed, burn it to return the Draconic Force to the Universe.

IV

Know Thyself

ဘာ

We have to learn what our capabilities and our limitations are. Recognizing ignorance is the beginning of knowledge. Learning to know oneself is the primary basis for perfecting one's knowledge, obtaining self-respect and from others, as well as spiritual upliftment and Draconic enlightenment. It also means we must be able to exercise good judgment and listen attentively to our intuition, as well as to our heart.

THIS Code statement states firstly that the dragon magician must be honest with himself so that he can accept and recognize his strengths as well as his weaknesses. Only by admitting that he's a constantly evolving Being will allow him to move faster on the magickal and spiritual path. Because indeed, knowing where our deficiencies are, allows us by then to take the appropriate course of actions and exercises required to achieve the perfect magickal balance. Putting one's focus in the right place also means putting aside certain more pleasant magickal practices, in favour of others that are more difficult to master, in order to attain a balanced structure of our person, our mind, our psychic senses and our draconic ideal.

Know thyself also means knowing how to respect yourself, to listen to your inner voice and to follow your intuition. The body knows what is good for him and it speaks to us. You have to listen carefully to hear his words. The following exercise should not be underestimated due to its simplicity. Because in reality, the daraco recognizes too well the strength of the techniques of meditation and visualization and will be able to benefit from them every time.

In Draconic Magick as in everyday life, we have an easy way to get to know ourself better. Indeed, introspection is undoubtedly a wonderful way to get to know who you are by taking silent journeys into your own consciousness. You will travel in your mind to bring out a situation that displeases you and that you would like to change. Once you have succeeded in isolating this discordant state, you will call on the appropriate dragon (which will have been chosen beforehand) so that he can teach you a way to address your current situation and make sure you get rid of it. It will therefore be important at this stage of the exercise to be very attentive and to remain passively open.

The messages received may not always be clear at first. Sometimes you will rather have impulses, feelings, new ideas, sensations, perhaps a sudden urge to do this or that, etc. Either way, go with the flow of your introspection and listen to your feelings. Let the dragon show you the way. At the end of the exercise, thank him for his help and note your results in your magickal diary. In time, you will come to interpret with more ease the messages that will have been transmitted by your draconic assistants.

In order to find the dragon that will most likely be of help during this magickal operation, here is a reminder of the dragon classes as well as some of their areas of expertise. You will find all the details and complete descriptions in Draconia. Please refer to it as needed. If in doubt, or if you cannot determine which Dragon Entity to summon, I recommend that you call on the guardian and protective dragons or your familiar dragon, if you already have one. These will always be of great help to you in all circumstances.

PECULIARITIES OF DRAGON CLASSES

Dragons of Forests & Mountains: Dragons of the Earth Element are favorable to all forms of esteem, depth, perseverance, punctuality, temperance and sense of responsibility. They help to establish solid and lasting foundations for all personal endeavors, to obtain stability, prosperity, endurance as well as personal strength. They help fight laziness, melancholy, heaviness, irregularity and disloyalty.

Dragons of Winds & Storms: Dragons of the Air Element help in developing intellectual and mental faculties, temperament, joy and pleasures, clarity and alertness of mind, skill, cordiality, optimistic attitudes , creativity, new ideas and concepts. They also deal with levity, boastfulness, talkativeness, presumptions, dissipation, frivolity, inattention and forgetfulness.

Dragons of the Seas & Aquatic Bodies: Dragons of the Water Element are good for causes of love and compassion, modesty, fervour, sobriety, peace, tranquillity and calmness, forgiveness and delicacy. They will help the magician in a better management of his emotions. They also deal with acts of indifference, insensitivity, phlegm, condescension, shyness, negligence and inconstancy and any other type of emotions.

Dragons of Magma & Volcanoes: Fire dragons grant willpower, strength, force, courage, activity, enthusiasm and determination. They will be of great help in effectively developing these qualities and can drastically sweep away all obstacles standing in the path of the practitioner. They also manage angry behaviour, anger, jealousy, hatred and revenge.

Great White Dragons: Light dragons are associated with light, Draconia, spirituality, spiritual awakening and upliftment, divine magick, the Sun, harmony, glory, truth, love, sharing, freedom, kindness in all its forms, indulgence, chivalry, purification of Karma, etc.

Great Black Dragons: Shadow dragons are associated with the same values as White dragons, but in their negative forms: shadow, misused of Draconia, density, fears, sleep and spiritual regression, negative magick, darkness, the Moon, conflict, loss, lies, despotism, burdening form karmic debts, etc.

Dragons of the Order: These dragons oversee order and balance, to start everything from anew and bring harmonious seeds to bloom. They help to hatch new projects, to stabilize them, to work on personal relationships, to improve all situations, even lost or hopeless causes. They offer the essential tools to move forward.

Dragons of Chaos: These dragons destroy wrong creations to build better ones. Bring about great changes, recreate lives, work within interpersonal relationships, change the flow of things, bring back luck, past lives, divinatory arts, eradicate toxic people and bad vibrations, break down physical and invisible obstacles.

Familiar Dragons: These dragons help with all matters of protection, security, inner peace, well-being and feelings of benevolence. They also promote all things related to love and friendship, divination, development of psychic powers as well as animals and pets.

*
**

Journey to the Center of Consciousness

Take your usual âsana or take a comfortable position, sitting or lying down. Make sure you are comfortable for a while. If desired, light a candle and play some relaxing music. Then close your eyes and take three deep breaths. Free your body and mind. Relax all your muscles. Now focus on your mind. Watch your wandering thoughts as they come and go for a short while, then put a stop to them and try not to think about anything at all. Pay attention to your breathing and let yourself be carried away by the stillness and silence of your own awareness.

After a few minutes, conjure up within yourself the image of a particular situation bothering you. In this regard, they can be lots of them. Do you suffer from a health problem or is there a situation at work that seems to be beyond your control? Do you lack concentration in your magickal practices or perhaps willpower? Find the subject of your concerns and project its image on your mental screen, then begin to study it from every angle without forcing anything, and silently ask the help of dragons, so they can discreetly whisper to you a solution. For example, if you have trouble concentrating, imagine an Air Dragon. See how it seems to hover in the air and swirl as it dances with the winds. Watch it wander here and there in graceful, calculated movements. Can this dragon help you gain more lightness in your thoughts? To become so graceful in your mind wanderings? To master what seems elusive and impalpable like the wind? Or, on the contrary, promote your concentration by reducing stray thoughts?

Ask him, mentally or aloud, to grant you inspiration to solve your current problem in words similar to these:

I ask Dragons to help me find,
The words and actions I must take.
Sprout in my mind the solution that suits me best,
So that this situation _____ can therefore end.
Ia! Draconis!
Ia! Draconia!

Let your mind follow the flow of your thoughts. Meditate on the images that your conscious and sub-conscious sends you. After about twenty minutes, return to your normal state of consciousness and end your meditation. In order not to calculate the time, you could put on some background music by choosing the duration of the tracks so that you know that when the relaxation music stops playing, you will know that you have practiced the exercise long enough. If necessary, write down any feelings in your magickal diary so you can follow your progress in this matter.

Value and Trust

හ⊙ශ

Fairness, honesty and loyalty will be part of the vital principles of the daraco. By expressing these qualities, he will gain not only the trust of dragons, but also that of his peers. Trust implies we are worthy and that our actions express a chivalrous attitude. The sharing of the High Draconic Knowledge is performed on the basis of these principles and the confidence that one acquires. This quality being recognized, dragons will accept the daraco with dignity as one of their own.

To be trustworthy towards our dragon guarantors; this is not always easy to do for a daraco. Unfortunately, sometimes, we cannot remain receptive to their suggestions (direct or subconscious) and that, as imperfect humans, we persist with impunity in following a path contrary or discordant without even realizing it.

Value and trust. The fifth Golden rule is, so to speak, the soul of the Draconic Code by its highly noble appearance and chivalrous qualities. This law resonates practically like the sparkling armor of a brave daraco. And metaphorically speaking, to wear an armor and represent the Draconia as a whole, it is still needed for the magician to be worthy of such a title. So it is important from time to time to visit our dragons, these dear co-magicians, through thoughts and words to strengthen the ties that bind us to them in Draconia.

The following draconic orison is a type of reverential prayer who will bring a spiritual state where your soul will be able to communicate through a meditative and contemplative state with the Draconic Force and his ministers. By uniting you to the whole Draconia by these words, you will also manage to raise and adjust your vibratory field, positioning yourself at the same frequency of the dragons.

As for the charge that you will find in the eleventh law of the Draconic Code, this prayer can be used daily during your magickal practices. It can be recited when you enter your magickal sanctuary or following the Draconic Cross, as an opening ritual or to close a dragon magick ceremony (providing an appropriate location if you practice the Major Rite of Opening and Closing) before, during or after a meditation, as a preliminary before embarking on a journey of consciousness in the Lair of Initiation, etc. These are only examples among many others, and the magician will have to once again rely on his sense of intuition and experimentation to determine how this prayer should be used.

Take your âsana or stand upright or on your knees. Take place before your altar, in front of a dragon image or statuette. In the absence of any of these objects, your Draconic Pentacle[8] will do the trick,

---

8   *Draconia*, p.71, Tools of Dragon Magick.

or even preferred, since this instrument of the Art should include at least a dragon effigy. Focus yourself for a short time and try to mentally establish contact with the Draconic Beings. Breathe deeply three times. Pose then your right hand on the heart and, in a clear voice, verbalize the prayer of the dragons.

***

Dragon Orison

Dragons of the Earth and Forests all around,
Dragons of the North on mighty ground.
Dragons of Winds, Storms and Air,
Dragons of the East, swift and fair.
Dragons of Water and Aquatic bodies,
Dragons of the West and magnetic Seas.
Dragons of Fire, Magma and Volcanoes,
Dragons of the South, burners of sorrows.
Great White Dragons, creatures of light,
Dragons of Spirit hear my plight.
Great Black Dragons, creatures of the night,
Dragons of Spirit, purifiers in might.
Dragons of Order, beneficial creatures,
Providers of purifying births so pure.

Dragons of Chaos, creatures of transformations,
Great destroyers of vile creations.
Guardian Dragons, Protectors in despair,
Watch over me and my humble lair.

(Give the Triple Sign)

Draconic Intelligences of all Realms,
Transcend your light in me through beams.
Draconic Beings, omnipotent Dragons,
Welcome into your ranks he who summons.
Dragons of the Elements and of starry wisdom,
My allegiance to you as I enter your kingdom.
Dragons from here and elsewhere,
Bless me now as I dare.

(Give the Triple Sign)

Fire of the First Flame burning bright,
Protect the Daraco by Soul and Light.
Breath of the Dragons, Great and Wise,
I humbly welcome your message.
Draconia, I welcome you, awake in me,
Draconia, I welcome you, shine through me.
Dragons of Knowledge, Wisdom and Heroic,
Teach me the Mysteries of your Sacred Magick.

(Give the triple sign)

Micama Vovina!
Ia! Draconis!
Ia! Draconia!

(Give the triple sign)

Act with Consciousness

෨෬

Just as dragons are sentient Beings, every action and ritual should be performed with this in mind. Dragon Magick must be practiced seriously and each magickal action should never be undertaken lightly, because the force drawn from within Draconia, is of such power, that it would be possible to wreak havoc from a misuse of draconic energies. This rule is closely related to the tenth rule of the Code.

THIS draconic statement teaches us that practicing Dragon Magick is not a hobby or a path taken solely for the sake of trying something new. Draconia is all serious. It is a path that promotes the global, magickal and spiritual development of the individual. It is a branch of the Holy Science of Magick that works closely with Dragon Entities. And it is in this sense that to act with conscience takes on its full meaning .

This sixth law is intimately linked to the tenth which is *Mastering Draconia*. To achieve an acceptable level of mastery, you must above all be able to deploy all the necessary efforts to achieve the goals that you have set yourself firsthand. Welcoming dragons into your daily life, meditating and conversing with them, following with commitment a structured approach and magickal training, all this goes hand in hand with this Golden rule.

Thus, both for the seasoned daraco as for the beginner magician, to act with awareness is something possible to achieve. But you still have to be able to awaken this same consciousness and to uplift it to a higher level. To show consciousness means to be aware to oneself, to our magician assistants and to one's immediate environment; it is to follow the path of wisdom and the dragons, it is to know how to get in tune with the Life that surrounds us and to bathe in the energies of the Cosmos and let them flow into us and through us.

If we wanted to sum it all up in a few words, we could synthesize that to be able to act consciously, we must be aware and attentive to our surroundings. And a good way to achieve this is to take a few moments a day to harmonize with the primordial Elements, which are the basis of all that exists.

It is important for a magician, whether draconic or other, to feel the connection that unites him to the Primordial Divine Source. Not only will this help him become aware the place he occupies in the Universe, but also to what level the macrocosm is exalted in the microcosm during his magickal practices. In everyday life, it is easy to become distracted and momentarily forget this connection between one's own inner divinity and that of the outer Higher Universe, the One. In order to reaffirm our magickal consciousness in this immensity and to focus our spiritual identity and individuality, it is possible to perform a gesture in order to confirm this perpetual link between Heaven and Earth, between Keter and Malkuth, between Divine Providence and his own Being, between the Draconia and the daraco.

Some magicians familiar with Western Ceremonial Magick practices already apply a semblance of magick gestures or, if you prefer, daily adorations, as they were taught and practiced by the GD[9]. Although having some similarities, these however differ from what is presented in this book in that they refer instead to the Sun as a symbol of light and life, which stands for the divine presence on Earth. On our side, in Draconia, we will rather opt for the symbolism of the four Elements as well as the classic position they occupy in their relationship with the four Watchtowers, in addition to various analogies, namely, the structure of the human body. I suggest that you start by familiarizing yourself with the gestures by reading the adoration as a whole, in order to understand the ties between the gestures and the vibrated words. You will quickly get a general understanding after a short study of the symbols in use.

---

9   Golden Dawn. *Liber Resh vel Helios*, after Aleister Crowley, is similar to the Adoration of the Four. However, this rite follows the course of the solar star through the day and the different cardinal points.

THE ADORATION OF THE FOUR

Stand in the center of your draconic sanctuary and face South. Stretch your arms out in front and form a triangle with your hands, pointing upward. That is to say that you will place your palms outward, thumbs against thumbs, index against index, the rest of the fingers folded, as shown in the figure opposite (Fig.3).

Focus your attention on the triangle. You are currently forming the symbol of the Element of Fire. Slowly bring the triangle up to your forehead. The head is the part of the body governed by this same Element. Inhale deeply and vibrate:

VOVIN–BITOM *(Voh-vee-neh-Bee-toh-meh)*

Extend your arms once more and contemplate your triangle of Fire for a short while. Then, place your arms alongside your body and pivot clockwise to stop facing East. You will therefore have to make an arc of 270 degrees on your axis.

Facing East, extend your arms and form a new upward-pointing triangle with your hands. Bring your attention to the triangle. You are now forming

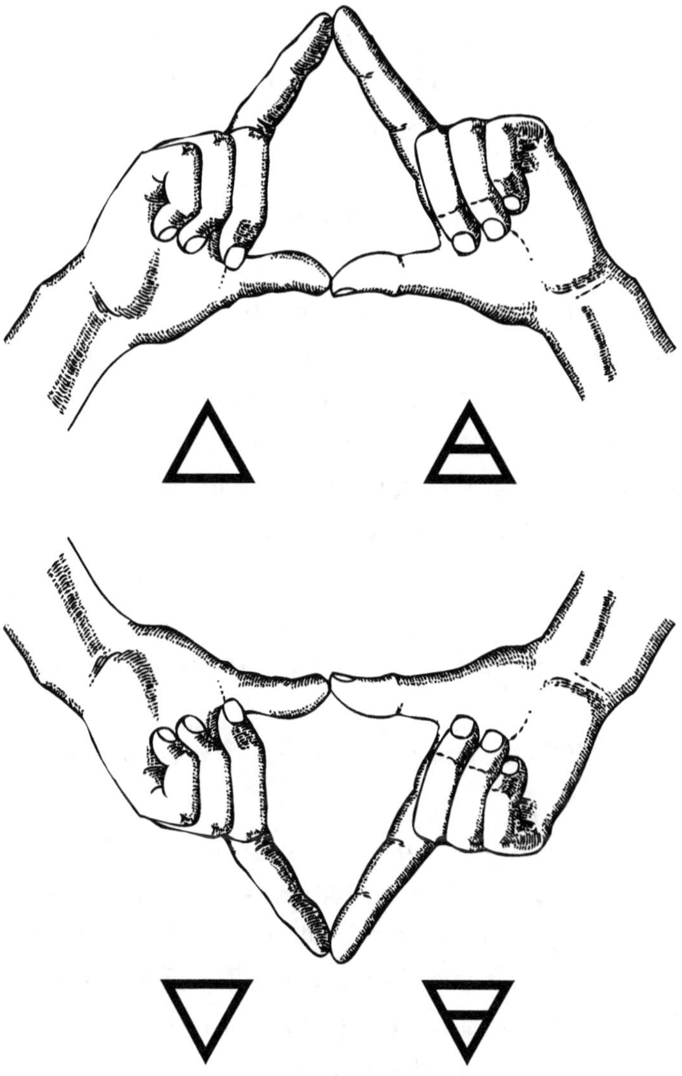

Figure 3.
Triangles of the Elements

the symbol of the Element Air, which also governs the region of the torso. Then bring the triangle up to your chest. Inhale deeply and vibrate:

VOVIN–EXARP *(Voh-vee-neh-Eht-zar-peh)*

Extend your arms once again and observe your Air triangle for a short time. Return your arms to your sides and rotate to stop facing West. Extend your arms and form a new triangle, this time pointing downward. This time, you are forming the symbol of the Element of Water, the same Element that governs the region of the lower body. Bring your attention to the triangle, then, bring it back to your lower abdomen. Inhale deeply and vibrate:

VOVIN–HCOMA *(Voh-vee-neh-Heh-coh-mah)*

Extend your arms once more and contemplate your triangle of Water. Then place your arms along your body and pivot so you'll stop facing North. Extend your arms and form a triangle, pointing down. You are currently forming the symbol of the Element of Earth, Element which governs the lower region and the legs. Stare at the triangle and bring it to the level of your navel. Inhale deeply and vibrate:

VOVIN–NANTA (*Voh-vee-neh-Nah-en-tah*)

Extend your arms one last time and observe your triangle of the Earth for a short moment. Bring the arms along the body, take a last deep breath. Exhale slowly. The ritual of the Adoration of the Four as come to an end.

You should normally repeat this adoration once a day, every day. Although it will take you very little time to practice, its application should not be under-estimated, which will have excellent effects on your magickal and mundane consciousness.

VII

Meditate and Converse

To meditate and converse with dragons is the way by which information is exchanged with magicians. Many messages are communicated during meditation sessions. To center oneself in silence, recollection and passivity will make it possible to perceive and obtain, sometimes even extraordinary, visions of things past, present or to come. Dragons use this language of communication mainly and almost exclusively. Meditation will therefore bring the daraco the necessary level of elevation, thus allowing familiar dragons or any other Draconic Being to converse directly with him in order to share information.

IN *Draconia*, my first book on Draconic Magick, it is explained in detail how the seventh rule of the Code *Meditate and Converse* is the technique most commonly used by daracos to exchange and communicate with dragons. It is also explained how the Draconic Beings, like all the Intelligences of the ethereal planes, will be able to capture the words, thoughts and feelings expressed by the practitioner. Just the fact of feeling an emotion will be enough to tint one's vibratory field, etheric body or, if you prefer, the aura. On another level, all these feelings or states of consciousness (love, hate, joy, compassion, etc.) become visible and easily interpreted by the inhabitants of these dimensions, including, of course, the Draconic Entities.

In the same way, by keeping an open mind and remaining in a state of passivity, not only will you be able to communicate your feelings, but more than that, you will be able to receive messages and emotional waves that dragons will communicate you in turn. By having previously developed your psychic senses, you will find out that it becomes rather easy to speak with Draconic Beings and many things will thus be unveiled. Meditation and contemplation bring the necessary level of elevation so that your familiar dragons, or any other Draconic Beings, can converse with you.

Never doubt your senses or the power of your visions under any circumstances. Know how to recognize the conversations you have had for what they are, that is to say, real experiences all the more authentic and sincere.

⁂

Meditation of the Draconic Crystal

Perform the Draconic Cross in your sanctuary to free your workspace from any residual energy. Then, if desired, light at least one candle and burn a sweet incense. Take on your usual âsana or sit comfortably and relax your whole body. Close your eyes, take three deep breaths and center yourself in silence.

Remember your initiation into Draconic Magick, if any, during your Rites of Passage in *vradysconns*. You have traveled by mind in the Draconic Zone, directly to find yourself in the *Lair of Initiation*. This is exactly where you will now return for this guided meditation.

Visualize that you are walking on a mild summer night. The sky is clear and starry, the air is warm and dry, you feel nice. The rays of a full moon illuminate a path marked by small stones from which emanates a faint white glow.

Take this path for a while, as you walk quietly, and look around. Everything is peaceful and quiet. The trail seems to be heading towards a rocky peak in the distance. Walk slowly until you reach the side of this mountain. Arriving at destination, you see the features of a cave in the shape of a large open mouth. It looks strangely like a dragon's head. You approach the entrance, take a short break, and then enter.

Once in the cave, you notice a tunnel disappearing into the bowels of the Earth. From there is a soft, soothing red glow. You take this slightly downwards sloping path that seems to disappear into the depths of human consciousness. As you walk down this descending slope, you feel more than ever the presence of dragons. Almost perceptible, they are not yet visible, but remain present. Your presence in this place has been noted and you know that, as a daraco living the Draconic Code with righteousness, you are welcome. You go deeper and deeper.

Gradually, you notice a change in the atmosphere. You are now wrapped in a reddish aura. This brightness is omnipresent and warm; this is the Draconic Force. It surrounds you, penetrates you and envelops you. You feel extremely calm, relaxed and at peace. You appreciate this state of bliss as you continue your descent on this path carved in stone. There are no visible lights or torches, yet you can see where you are putting your feet in this soft glow that looks as impalpable as the ambient air.

Finally, after a slow descent that seems to have lasted for quite some time, right in front of you, at the end of the tunnel, stands a huge silver door. It is rounded up in an arc shape. It looks thick and solid, as if made of pure solid silver. Surprisingly, as soon as you push it, it opens easily without making any noise and immediately lets through a bright light momentarily dazzling, as if for a moment you were looking directly at a blinding sun.

As your eyes become accustomed to the light, you walk the threshold to find yourself in a large circular room carved out of the stone. The ceiling is very high. The walls are adorned with long purple red tapestries that evoke dragons of various sizes in strange movements. You know too well where you are. You are now in the heart of Draconia or, at least, in one of its many material representations, that are only known and accessed the daracos.

The presence of dragons is felt more than ever; they are very close to you. In the center of the room is a beautiful ruby-colored soft carpet with silver edges. In front of the latter, you can see a small stone block resembling an altar on which rests a crystal or a transparent stone.

You are slowly approaching the altar. You humbly give the Triple Sign and take the crystal. Then you go to the center of the carpet and sit there. As you contemplate the crystal in your hands, you notice that it is warm to the touch and seems to have an almost hypnotic effect on your soul and consciousness. It seems to bear some kind of engravings, but at the moment, you cannot properly distinguish them or understand their meaning. It looks like you were holding a translucent quartz with red veins or would it be a red quartz with pale veins? It seems like its appearance is constantly changing, as if it were a living being in your hands. You hold it firmly against your chest, almost as if you wanted to protect it, as if it were the most precious of objects, then, you close your eyes and slowly sink into a trance state...

*****

The rest of this meditation belongs to you. Unfortunately, I cannot guide you any further. The way you'll use the crystal is also up to you. Will you have to draw magickal, kabalistic or rune symbols in the air? Will a dragon come to you to teach you any art or magick? Whatever this may be, this crystal is there for you and the dragons will know how to use it. Let your intuition guide you and let the Draconic Beings communicate to you the information they deem relevant to your personal, magickal or spiritual development.

When you're done conversing with the dragons, put the crystal back in place, leave the circular room and silently walk back to the surface. Under no circumstance should you forget to put the instrument back in place before you leave. Once outside, stop and see if there's any dragon waiting for you to give you a final message. Then, open your eyes, and go back to your normal state of consciousness.

VIII

INVOKE OFTEN

෫)෬

Dragons know how to listen to draconic magicians who have forged special bonds with them. Invoke your winged assistants, invoke them often! He who never asks for anything will never receive anything. On the other hand, whoever asks for the dragons' help and invokes them will be heard and even answered, provided that his requests are just and valid and do not contradict the laws that govern the Universe. A daraco will never underestimate dragons because he recognizes their remarkable qualities, their might and the help he is able to receive from them.

THIS very simple ritual comes from the first tome Draconia. It seemed more than obvious to me that the latter should be included as the eighth rule. So instead of trying to reinvent the wheel, I decided to share it with you in this book, as it was presented earlier. In order to receive the daily help of the Draconic Beings and their blessing, formulate your requests regularly. And in terms of invocation, here you have the perfect formula to call the dragons. It is a very short, simple call, and can be made at any time and under any circumstances.

Make this invocation every day, preferably when you get up, when you go to bed, or better yet, on both occasions, at first when you getting up in the morning and just before you retire for the night. It will take you no more than a few seconds to put into practice and it will allow you to better start and conclude your day. It is an invocation that you will send toward the Draconic Force in order to strengthen this bond that unites you in Draconia. It will be favorable to you to succeed in raising yourself and tuning your vibratory field at the same frequency as that of the dragons. Conclude by giving the Triple Sign, as you are now used to do.

DAILY DRAGON INVOCATION

Place your right hand on your heart and say in a clear voice:

Awake, O noble and mighty Draconic Force,
Awake in me and shine through my whole being!
O breath of the Dragons, Great and Wise,
Make my spirits a vessel of Truth.
Offer me your Knowledge and Wisdom,
And teach me the Mysteries of your Magick.
I welcome all the Dragons in my heart and soul,
And may we work together for the Draconia!
Bless me among yours,
And lead me to perfection.
O noble Draconic Force, omnipotent Dragons,
Manifest yourself in me and radiate through my being!
Manifest, Manifest, Manifest!
Shine, shine, shine!
Draconis, draconis, draconis!

Give the Triple Sign.

IX

The Science of Goodness

ଽଚ

Draconia is, above all, the ultimate knowledge and power of dragons. This esoteric science is oriented mainly towards knowledge, personal development and magickal practices, goodness, action of elementary energies and defense. It is never employed for provocation or direct magickal attacks. Sometimes, and on rare occasions, an attack may seem like the best defense you have. But that depends on the circumstances. At that point, the judgment will be questioned. It is imperative that the daraco comply with this rule, otherwise he may lose the draconic guides and assistants he has been granted.

The statement of the ninth Golden rule highlights knowledge, wisdom and magickal development. This is exactly what the following practice will aim for; to stimulate learning and promote the daraco's development by circulating the vital force. In order to become even more efficient in Draconic Magick, you will learn to create a powerful charge of spiritual energy that can, in much the same way as when you accumulate the Draconic Force, be used for different goals in practical magick. Those who are already versed in Ceremonial Magick techniques will undoubtedly notice a similarity with the Middle Pillar Ritual.

The MPR is what we might call one of the basic rituals in the ceremonial magician's arsenal. The framework of this rite will remain unique and always as effective, no matter how it is applied. What I understood from its practice was that this exercise would remain beneficial to the magician, regardless of whether the ritual is performed silently, with the use of Hebrew, Enochian or other names. To this end, it is possible to preserve the base of the Middle Pillar and incorporate it into our daily Draconic Magick by substituting the traditional Hebrew names for a mix of Enochian/Draconic. We thus succeed in personalizing an exceptional ritual by adjusting it more intimately to the frequency that interests us here, that is, that of the dragons. At the end of the ritual, you will find a table containing the correspondence of the magick names used as well as their associations with the Sephirots of the Kabbalistic Tree of Life and their French equivalent.

By practicing this ritual on a regular basis, you will be able to balance your psychic centers, generate, direct and control the magickal energy, use it to charge any object, talisman or place of your choice, etc. Great achievements can be expected by working with this energy current. Even exceptional. Moreover, repeating this ritual seriously and thoroughly on a daily basis will greatly contribute to the development of your psychic senses. As additional benefits, its practice will also bring you greater stability, vitality and mastery of the Magickal Arts. Thus, pay particular attention to the Draconic Pillar. The efforts you will put into its practice will soon pay off.

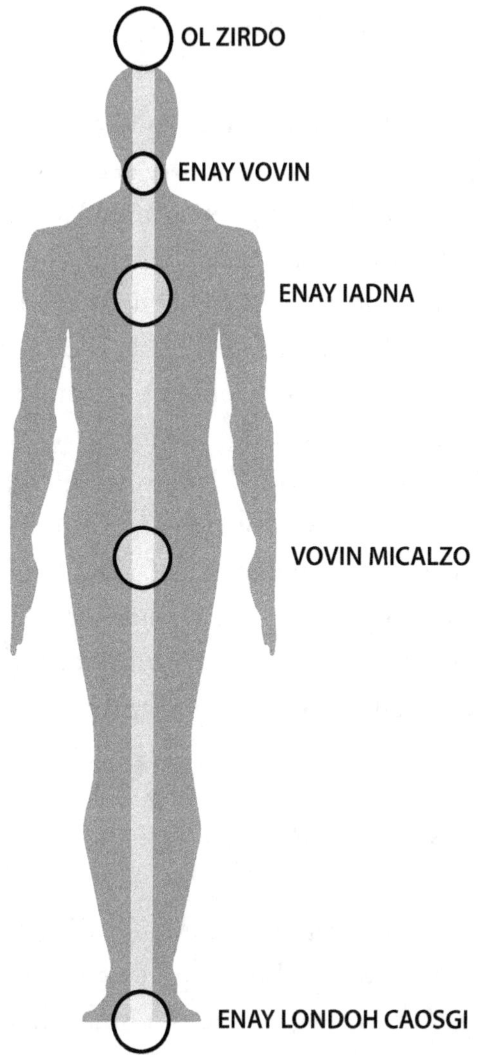

Figure 4.
The Draconic Pillar

The Draconic Pillar

Perform the Draconic Cross. Following this Major Rite, you are now standing in the center of a circle of light circled with four Pentagrams. Pay attention to the sphere of light above your head, the same as during the Draconic Cross. This light is extremely bright, white and pulsating; This is the Primordial Divine Source, the One. Contemplate it for a moment in a state of increased passivity.

Point it with your index finger of your right hand and draw down a beam of light to your forehead. This establishes the connection of your Higher Self to the Divine. Be aware of this connection. Then vibrate the following name three times and see how the sphere becomes brighter and pulsating on each reiteration:

OL ZIRDO *(Oel Zodiredo)*

Then visualize a light beam descending from the sphere above your head to stop at your throat. See a second sphere of light, though smaller, forming there. The two spheres are connected by a column of white bright light. While becoming aware that this link symbolizes the union between your Supreme Self and your Conscious Self, the second sphere begins to become pulsating and increases in brightness. Vibrate the following name three times and see how the sphere reacts by becoming brighter and pulsating during this verbalization:

ENAY VOVIN (*Enayo Vovini*)

While maintaining the image of the previous spheres in your mind, visualize the beam of light continuing its descent from the sphere at your throat to stop and form a third bright sphere at your solar plexus. This sphere of light becomes more intense as you understand that it symbolizes your consciousness. Vibrate the following name three times and notice how the sphere becomes brighter and pulsating with each repeated verbalization:

ENAY IADNA (*Enayo Iadinah*)

Visualize the column of light descending even lower, along your body to stop at your navel. A fourth sphere of light forms there. Recognize yourself as the master of your Lower Self, who was once guided by his instincts. Vibrate the following name three times and see how the sphere becomes brighter and more pulsating during this verbalization:

VOVIN MICALZO (*Vovini Mikalazodo*)

Lower the beam of light to your feet. Here will be formed the last sphere that will encompass both your feet and beneath them, as if the sphere of light were half under the ground. Vibrate the following name three times and observe how the sphere becomes brighter and more pulsating during this verbalization:

ENAY LONDOH CAOSGI (*Enayo Elonudohe Caosâji*)

In peace and silence, contemplate the spheres connected to each other by the column of light. You just created the Draconic Pillar. Stay in this state for as long as you want. When you decide it's time to close the ritual, take a deep breath and, when you exhale, visualize the spheres and the column of light slowly fade away and disappear. They will no longer be visible, but will still be present.

Sephira	Enochian	Meaning
Keter	OL ZIRDO	I am
Daath	ENAY VOVIN	Lord Dragon
Tipheret	ENAY IADNA	Lord *of* Knowledge
Yesode	VOVIN MICALZO	Dragon almighty
Malkuth	ENAY LONDOH CAOSGI	Lord *of the* Earthly Kingdom

Table 2.
Sephiroth/Enochian correspondences

 X

MASTERING DRACONIA

ℰᏩᏘ

Mastering the microcosm to make changes within the macrocosm means being able to control yourself and achieve mastery of one's self. Mastery is the ultimate path to follow when one profoundly seeks external results through Dragon Magick. Controlling our own small universe, in order to bring about change within the Great Universe, is to understand and effectively apply the principles of Draconia that will make the daraco a respected and powerful Draconic magician.

THE draconic magician recognizes that he is a microcosm interacting within the macrocosm. He is a perfect little universe to himself among a multitude of other universes as complete and defined as he is, and all interacting within a larger and infinite scheme, the great universe. This interpretation of grandeur and proportion which we would define as the state of absolute relativity between Beings is important when we look at the person we are and the place we occupy within our environment, our society, our city, our nation, the material plane, the invisible planes, the Heavenly Hierarchy, etc.

I explain in my magickal training *La Science des Mages*[10] this very important concept with a simple analogy. Imagine a beautiful mature tree all in leaves. At first glance you might infer that it has a unique and robust trunk and leafy branches. If you look closer, you will notice that each branch, every shoot

---

10 *La Science des Mages: Traité Initiatique de Haute Magie,* Unicursal 2016.

as small as it is, is made in the same way. Another smaller trunk, other smaller branches, etc. It could be said that a tree is made up of several small trees living together, thus forming a larger tree, several unique microcosms living in symbiosis within a perfect whole, a representation of a single tree, a single universe or macrocosm.

From a different perspective, we can safely say that we are all one, small, complete Universe living within another Universe, which is endless and infinite. And by this very fact, that every man and woman is a star. Several unique and individual stars orbiting a single Universe.

In order for the draconic magician to be able to express the tenth law of the Code and to succeed in mastering Draconia as well as to succeed in producing changes in his immediate surroundings, he must first be able to master himself. It is imperative that he be able to master his own inner Universe before aspiring to master the outer Universe. How can a practitioner of the Art aspire to change all around him if he is not even able to control himself and make changes within himself? This is simply impossible in magick and this explains why many people do not achieve any satisfactory degree of success in practical or Draconic Magick.

When aspiring to become a true and powerful magician, it is essential to practice exercises of mastery and personal development. Once in full control of the microcosm, the daraco knows that he will be able to bring about changes within the macrocosm, which will always be in accordance with its will.

The following exercise expresses admirably the tenth Golden rule of the Draconic Code. You will learn to accumulate the Draconic Force in your body and shape it in accordance with your will, in order to develop qualities that will strengthen your magickal mastery skills in Draconia.

⁎⁎⁎

A Draconic Mastery

In your magickal temple, take a sitting position that will not cause you any discomfort. If you are already accustomed to taking an âsana, then go ahead with it. Then close your eyes and visualize yourself in the center of the Universe. You can see stars and galaxies all around you. You feel this grandiose vastness. Then pay attention right in front of you where there is now a beautiful golden red shimmering and pulsating sphere. Approach slowly until it is very close. You are impressed by its size, as it seems to be at least five times your own size. This sphere of energy is the visual representation of the Draconic Force in the raw state. It irradiates in all directions a warm and bright energy. You understand that this sphere is extremely powerful and that it would be impossible for you, for all practical purposes, to contain it all, as its energy seems titanic. When you are able to visualize the whole scene as clearly as if you were looking at it with your physical eyes, continue the exercise.

Now, by conscious pore breathing, in the same way as a sponge one would dip into the water, absorb this energy through all the pores of your skin. Imagine as you deeply breathe in, that a light beam is transferred from the sphere of draconic energy, directly into you, through your whole body. The latter then becomes a receptacle which, little by little, accumulates this light energy in it. The more you inhale the Draconic Force, the more your body reacts to its contact and becomes almost translucent as it strongly irradiates the accumulated energy.

In doing so, while your body absorbs and compresses this force, charge its light with a defined and precise quality, such as perseverance, patience or control; in short, one of the qualities required to achieve a balance tending towards magickal mastery. For example, you could opt for the same quality you had previously chosen when exercising your morning introspection and Draconic charge, in the third statement of the Code.

When you breathe out, nothing should be expelled from your body. The draconic energy will remain in you permanently. Breathe in again and, while charging it with the chosen quality, keep accumulating the Draconic Force, seeing it penetrate you from everywhere until you feel that this energy is compressed to a degree that you cannot take anymore, like a balloon almost too swollen that would be about to burst. The entire process should take a total of more or less thirty consecutive inhalations, without counting them.

Now that you are fully charged, focus on the quality previously chosen and see how, thanks to the Draconic Force, it comes to be impregnated in your astral body, there to be transferred and ready to manifest itself. To achieve this, visualize, for example, that your body's outline is made up of a diaphanous and shiny membrane (your astral envelope) and see how it adopts the hue and radiance of accumulated energy.

Take as much time as you want to bathe in this beneficial energy. Then, when you are convinced that you have properly transferred the charge into you, it will be time to expel the Draconic Force out of your body. It is very important to never forget to release the accumulated light, otherwise you may feel overloaded and find it difficult to function normally, as if you had drunk a dozen strong coffees.

Instead of simply discharging the accumulated energy, you will use it to impregnate your immediate surroundings. The method of transferring out this powerful energy, now compressed in your body, will be by *indirect induction*; that is by expiration through the solar plexus.

The transfer of the Draconic Force via the solar plexus is the most appropriate method for any type of indirect charge. It is a general charge, such as impregnating a place, the effects of which will be felt by all those in the visible or invisible vicinity, whether it be humans or Entities. This transfer will take place in much the same way as before, but in reverse.

Breathe deeply and then breathe out slowly. When you exhale, visualize the Draconic Force expelling itself through your solar plexus, like a jet of light or vapor escaping from your body to impregnate the room where you are. Have the certainty that the place will vibrate the projected quality. Breath in again, without visualizing anything, then breathe out and visualize the energy leaving your body, bit by bit, and transfer itself in the atmosphere. You should normally use as many exhalations to transfer this Force from your body as there were breathings to accumulate it in you. Once you have rejected all the light energy, the practice of Draconic mastery will be fully completed.

By following my instructions correctly, you will have managed to accomplish two very distinct things at the end of the exercise. First, you will have accumulated the Draconic Force in your body, charging it with a precise quality. That quality will then have been transferred into your psychic body in order to plant there the desired charge, which can accomplish its work without you having to pay attention to it afterwards. As a result, you also have subsequently expelled the same force outside your body to impregnate the astral of your workplace so that the charge will be able to manifest itself there, and radiate on you the same quality that it has been imbued with.

You will not only have worked at your own magickal and Draconic mastery, but more than that, you will have managed to generate and control a flow of energy, a particular vibration whose effects will be felt at different levels of yourself.

XI

Preserving and Teaching Draconia

ഓരു

It is the daraco's duty to preserve first and foremost the Draconic heritage and to pass it on to his relatives who share the same love for the dragons, and in whom he has complete confidence. By keeping this precious knowledge intact, which has resisted the erosion of time so well, Draconia will continue to radiate and illuminate the hearts of all practitioners of this marvelous discipline and esoteric tradition for centuries to come.

THE Charge of the Dragon is a sacred text because of its great symbolism. It represents the declaration made by the First Dragon unto the daracos. Just as a deity would do to his disciples, the voice is that of a Draconic Entity, a dragon of the First Flame, which transmits its message to all draconic magicians, as taught by the eleventh and last Golden rule of the Code.

This charge can be used in many ways and applied daily during your Draconic Magick. It can be recited aloud when you enter your magickal sanctuary or to mark the beginning and end of your meetings with your daracos brothers and sisters, if you are a member of a group or convent. You can recite it as a ritual opening to establish contact with the dragon Entities or, on the opposite, to close a ceremony, before, during, or after a meditation, as a preliminary before embarking on a journey of consciousness in the Lair of Initiation, etc. These are just examples among many others and the magician will once again have to rely on his sense of intuition and experimentation to determine how to use this important text when he moves forward to the practical part of Draconia.

****

The Charge of the Dragon

Hear the dragon rising and standing in this sanctuary. See it stand tall and straight. Feel its power and strength. See his eternal wisdom through the ages! Whether he is white or black, of shadow or light, of the Earth, of the Air, of Water or of Fire, whether he destroys or purifies, whether he blesses and cherishes or rejects and breaks, hear the supreme voice of the dragon.

I am the dragon of the desert stone, of woods and forests,
I was born from the North, from the cold and the iron.
I am the dragon of the cloudy peaks where the terrible
    winds blow,
I was born from the East, from the heavens and the at-
    mosphere.
I am the dragon of the resonant seas, of the lakes and
    rivers,
I was born from the West, from the depths and the seabed.

I am the dragon of the bowels of fire and of impetuous
    volcanoes,
I was born from the South, from the rage and blood of
    the earthly veins.
I am the dragon of eternal and shining light,
I was born from the Cosmos among the stars.
I am the dragon of darkness and shadowy night,
I was born out of chaos that created me.
I am the dragon of balance and renewal.
I was born to the childbearing giver.
I am the destructive dragon and of fatality,
I was born of wars and from the violence of peoples.
I'm the dragon watching over you and your loved ones,
I was born of benevolence and shining armor.

Come, haste and listen, says the dragon to the daracos
who come before the Draconia in this sacred Temple.
Come to me, O Universal Creatures. Haste at my call, O
Draconic Beings. Listen and hear my voice, O dragon
Entities.

I am the Flame of the First Flame,
I am the Breath of the First Breath.
I am the Wings in the night,
And the Crown during the day.

I am the Fire that delivers and consumes,
I am the Master of the Magickal Arts.

Come, haste and listen, for I am the dragon who bears the whole Draconia in this sacred Temple. Come to me, O Universal Creatures. Haste at my call, O Draconic Beings. Listen and hear my voice, O dragon Entities. Draconic acts are my rituals for I am what is achieved at the end of the day of life.

Draconis, draconis, draconis!

The Eleven Draconic Seals

THE ELEVEN DRACONIC SEALS

ELEVEN are the Golden rules of the Draconic Code and eleven are the Seals associated with it. Among the practical applications of the Code in Magick, there is a technique that makes it possible to precipitate and sublimate the very essence of this dragon convention by means of special Sigils called *Draconic Seals*.

These power glyphs, so to speak, represent the energetic and subtle Force, the vibrational ideology behind the rules of the Draconic Code. Acting by analogy as batteries, they must be charged so that they can then dispense their power to the magician. These Sigils are, in a way, receptacles and capacitors of Heavenly energies, physical and concrete representations in this present, material plane of ours.

The proper function of these magickal symbols is to channel and radiate through the body of the daraco, just as in its immediate environment, this essence of wisdom conveyed by the rules of the Draconic Code. This technique will therefore allow him to ennoble his character by creating a vibratory adjustment by means of an occult symbol representing a Force, a particular message through his own structure, aura and vibratory field. We therefore understand here that this means, among other things, to charge one's etheric and astral body. In other words, just as if one were to synthesize the love he would like to receive and experience in return for another person, by materializing on a piece of paper the shape of a heart as a symbol, the operator who will draw the Seals representing these cosmic energies will know how to create powerful emitters of draconic vibrations, in order to impregnate himself with them. He will therefore radiate this Force through his vibratory field, positively affecting in the way all Being around him at the same time, in the same way as would a walker in the middle of the night equipped with a powerful lantern. There will be many benefits for the magician in performing this technique, there is absolutely no doubt, since it is a proven technique.

With the help of the Seals in this book, it will also be possible to manifest a draconic vibratory Force which is highly beneficial to the user, simultaneously on all three planes of existence, namely the mental, astral and material plane. Not only will he be more in tune with the statements that make up the Dragon Code, but even more visible changes in everyday life can be expected and actually perceived.

Of course, in order to achieve such a degree of success on the three planes, it must nevertheless be expected that the results obtained will always be in analogy with the magickal development of the operator, namely whether the latter is well trained beforehand. In any case, practice and perseverance are qualities known to the draconic magician and the latter recognizes the strength of his will as a powerful ally in the practice of his Draconia workings.

The aware student will notice from reading the following that the way this technique of Magick works is somewhat similar to the precepts of Ceremonial Magick, which is referred to by evocations; certainly, much more complex, but at the same time similar in some respects. magickal evocations works with different types of Entities and involve bringing different classes of Spirits, Intelligences or demons to physical manifestation on the material plane. Although the latter practice requires extremely rigorous training and serious personal preparation, the magickal practice of Seals, despite several similarities, is not dangerous and will instead call upon global Draconic Forces (or more abstract and not necessarily having defined forms, if I may say so) in the sense that these will be rather real qualities or energetic currents but not Entities or Intelligences coming from the invisible Realms.

Thus, just as magick evocations aims the physical manifestation of an Entity, that is to say, that we call forth a Spirit living on a higher plane and bring it on our own dimension, it will be possible for the operator to bring to him a manifestation of an energy or vibration (or even of a thought-form which would here possess a body, a mental or astral shell according to its level of intensity) which will be in perfect analogy with a specific desire, and this, also, on the physical plane. Namely, channeling a subtle Force residing in the cosmos that will be brought to oneself voluntarily by a magickal act.

If this seems a little complicated to you, or if my explanations seem complex, let me simply summarize what was said by repeating my previous example with love, that instead of aiming at a specific person to come to love us, by drawing a heart, it is rather to bring to oneself the feelings of love, the sensual love energy and to manifest it in order to be imbued with it, without specifying a specific person and to let the Universe take charge of the rest.

*
**

Different types of Seals

At it is, and for all types of magick combined, a Seal is a graphical and physical embodiment of an Entity, an Intelligence or even an elemental, energetic or universal Realm. It is a type of occult signature representing a unique whole, a condensed and precise Force. We find in the magician's arsenal various types of Seals including:

1. Traditional Seals — There are different types of magickal Seals. Among these we find the traditional ones representing Entities, Spirits, angels or demons, as in the case of magickal evocations. Excellent examples can be found in Ceremonial Magick texts such as *Goetia* or the *Clavicles of Solomon*. These Spirits have generally revealed their signatures or magickal characters by themselves to the magician, unless, of course, the magician has captured them by clairvoyance. Like a business card, these Seals will be used to call the Entity to show itself to the magician in order to communicate and exchange on different topics or to perform some occult work.

2. *Universal Seals* — We then have Seals that will be used to express certain aspects or qualities from a given Intelligence. For example, in the case of a Spirit known to bring ease of learning, a Seal could be made to manifest these qualities and thus improve its user in the study of his Art. In other words, a Seal that does not represent the Entity itself, but rather one of its offices or areas of expertise.

3. *Seals of energetic Realms* — Finally, we have the Seals that will represent qualities specific to a given domain, without being associated with a specific Entity. It is then a magickal signature effective in being the representation of the elemental, energetic or universal type. In the context of Draconic Magick, it is exactly this type of Seals that we will use. The latter will not therefore be associated with a particular dragon, nor any Kabbalistic Spirit or Genii, but rather with an energetic Realm, an ideology, a very precise quality or, as far as we are concerned, a rule of the Draconic Code.

It will indeed be possible to capture the essence of an impalpable Force or idea, graphically, and physically. We know that everything in the Universe is energetic and vibratory. From there, knowing that on another more subtle plane, an action, an idea, a quality can be perceived as a sound, a color or a form, it then becomes possible to precipitate this energy by condensing it into a physical form representing a much larger and stronger ideal.

And so, it is with these explanations that the daraco will be able to design, charge and use various Seals and symbols, in order to create a physical embodiment, directly tied to a Draconic Force, that he will awaken and bring to manifestation in his magickal sanctuary.

*
**

Of the making of Seals

There are many different ways to make the Seals used in Magick, from the simplest to the most complex processes. Traditionally, the image is etched onto a metal in analogy with the plane of existence from which the Entity originates or the Realms it has to represent. Therefore, the magician would use gold for the Solar Realm, silver for the Moon, copper for Venus, iron for Mars, etc. Without a metal support, the operator would then use pure beeswax plates that he had made himself or, as in the present case, virgin parchment.

If it were, say, a planetary intelligence, then the use of parchment would be effective in conjunction with inks of the color analogous of that Realm. The goal is always to exalt as much as possible the very essence of the chosen Realm. In this order, for a Seal under the Martians offices or for the Fire Element, a red ink would be used. In the same way, one would use a blue ink to correctly express the Jupiter Realm, green for Venus and so on, always following this same way of correspondences.

Although a metal support is preferable for a long-term Seal, virgin parchment is an extremely suitable substitute because of its low cost and ease of working. That's what we're going to use for our Magick work in this chapter. Since the ideals conveyed by the Draconic Code are not of planetary or elementary origin, the color of the ink to be used will therefore be neutral, or black.

To make your Draconic Seals, start by purifying your raw materials. Take a blank piece of parchment paper and free it from any undesired influence. Do the same with your pen and inks. I suggest that you purify them following the practice of the Draconic Cross by using the light produced by this Major Rite to exorcise them and chase away any psychic filth. And so it's done; it shouldn't be more complicated than that. Your material is now ready for use.

Then carefully draw the desired Seal and let the ink dry. Once completed, you will move on to the next step; the charge. Just as a flat battery would require you to be charged before being used, without the charge, your magick Sigil will, alas, produce no noticeable effect. Therefore, pay special attention to the following procedure.

*
**

Of the Triangle of Manifestation

In order to manifest the Seals on the physical plane, the magician will place the latter in the center of a triangle, the upper point pointing upwards, which he himself will have built for this purpose.

The triangle is a form evoking the three-dimensional world, that is, it's a perfect representation of the mental, astral and physical world. It symbolizes the world of causes in manifestation. It will therefore not be surprising to understand why the triangle is expressed in all things and on every plane of existence, since it is the basis of every creation and every manifestation.

Since everything that manifests here below on the material plane must necessarily start a descent from the higher planes, to the physical one (mental, astral, material), it is customary to use a triangle in order to precipitate a Force from the mental and astral planes. The daraco will take the time to understand and study the symbolism of the triangle in order to know its many implications in Magick.

On a practical side, the triangle may be made of fabric, cardboard, wood or any other material that is deemed suitable. There is no rule except that the equilateral triangle will be favored over the others because of its three equal sides. The size will be considered suitable as long as the Seals can be placed in its center without difficulty as shown (Fig. 5) and the latter can rest properly on your altar. Triangles that are too small or too large will be avoided. Generally, a triangle with sides about 30 centimeters long would do just fine. A material that is easy to use and reuse during subsequent draconic practices would also be a good thing to keep in mind when making it, because indeed, the triangle of manifestations will be called upon to serve on many occasions. To give you a start-

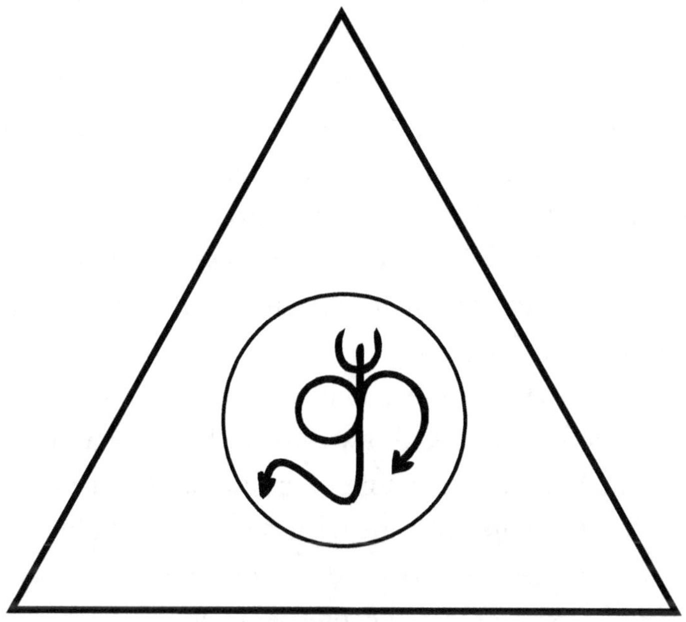

Figure 5.
Triangle of Manifestation

er idea of how to build your triangle, a thin wooden model with a white background and a black circle in the center would be excellent, as well as being robust enough to last for many years.

Of the Charge of the Seals and their Use

The daraco who wishes to benefit from the influences of the Draconic Seals will use the procedure that I will now explain. This will be identical for all Seals contained in this work.

Take a seat in the center of your magickal temple and perform the Draconic Cross, if it has not been done before during the purification of your materials. Indeed, if you decide to charge your Seal at a later time, it would be, at the very least, a great idea to practice that Major Rite again before proceeding with the charging process.

All these considerations aside and once your parchment, pen, ink and workplace have been properly sanitized, stand before your altar and place your Seal in the center of your triangle. You can light two candles placed on each side, if desired. Then take three deep breaths and center yourself.

Recite the Charge of the Dragon (*Law XI*).

Then recite the Daily Dragon Invocation (*Law VIII*).

Now that your calls to the Draconic Force have been duly made, realize the significance of the triangle of manifestation; the latter represents the causes that will come to manifest on the material plane. Then, using your wand (if you have your magickal tools) or your index finger, trace the outlines of the triangle physically, mentally and mentally, while keeping in mind the very high symbolism of this diagram. Stay deeply focused throughout this process.

Now, pay attention to the center of the triangle. Gaze the Seal in front of you and establish a connection with its symbolism. For example, in the case of the 10th Draconic Seal, it would then be the Golden rule meaning to *Master Draconia*. Focus on this Draconic Code rule and meditate on its profound meaning for a few minutes.

Then, just as you did for the triangle, trace the Seal physically, psychically and mentally, always using your wand or index finger, while keeping in mind all the qualities that this image represents. You will then impregnate the Seal by means of visualization by running through it one line at a time. As you do, see it react and come to life in the form of a glowing light, much like a neon sign that you light up, just like if you were tracing over it with a welding torch, in the same way as when you visualize the Pentagrams when you perform the Draconic Cross.

Keep gazing your Seal with intensity. See the lines vibrate with brightness, as if the glyph on the parchment was now alive and pulsating in intensity as it follows your own pulse, making one with each of your breaths. Try to make this contact with your deep psyche. Visualize this symbol transcending into you and throughout your being. You only see this Seal, you become this draconic symbol, you now become this image, this Force, this vibration. When you feel you have done it right, give the Triple Sign. The procedure has been completed.

Once you have done so, know that your Seal has been duly charged and that it really contains the power that has been impregnated with. You now have a magickal tool manifesting a Draconic Force on the mental, astral and, if everything was done properly according to the directives, undoubtedly on the material plane.

From here, you have two choices. You can either wear the Seal on yourself, for a period of at least seven consecutive days or more. You will place it in a silk pouch of white or black color. Otherwise, you can simply store it in your magickal cabinet for reuse during a new charging session or, again, place it in the center of your home to benefit from its effects. Ideally, you should carry the Seal on you at all times, just as you would with a talisman, so that you can always benefit from its influence repeating the charge process from time to time, at regular intervals. Since its emission range is short, if you are not in the presence of the Seal, you will not be able to benefit from its effects, in the same way that you would not be able to smell the scent of incense if you are far away from it.

Either way, when you decide it is time to discard your Seal, you will go back in your draconic sanctuary to dissolve it and send it back to the Universe. To do this, just burn the parchment and dispose of the ashes properly.

Before undertaking any draconic Seal endeavor, I recommend that you write down your preparations in your magickal diary. Take note of everything that seems relevant to you, such as the Seal evoked, the date of creation, the date of dissolution, the lunar phase, the temperature, your current physical condition, whether you are in good shape, tired or suffering from discomfort, how you felt after evoking your Seal, etc. Later, you will be happy to compare your notes. They will help you validate your failures as well as your successes.

First Seal

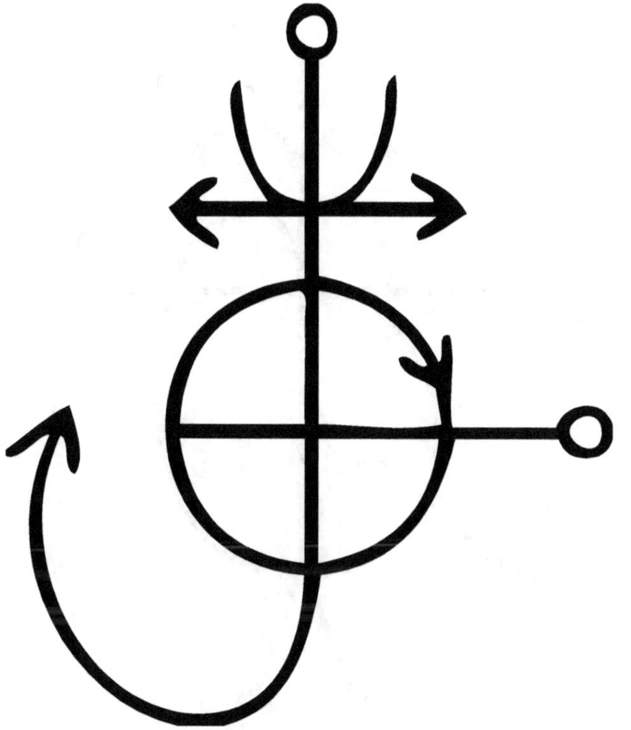

Deep Respect of Dragons

SECOND SEAL

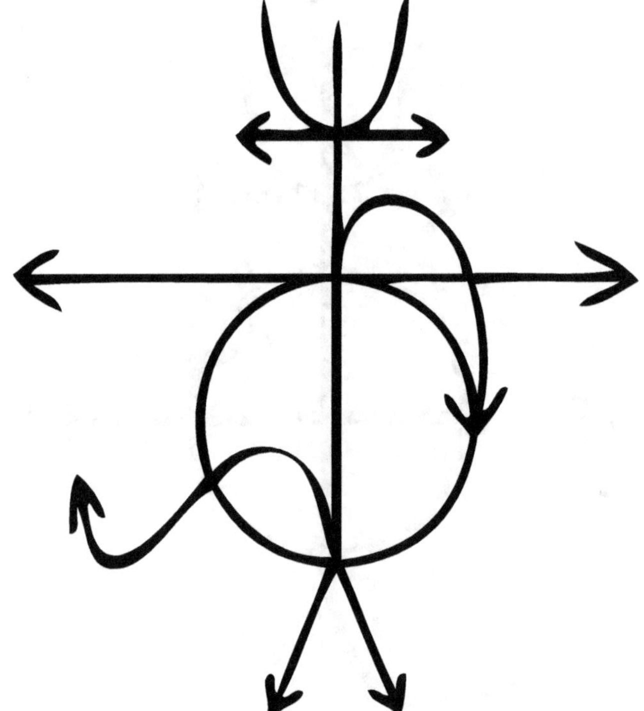

RESPECT FOR UNIVERSAL CREATURES

THIRD SEAL

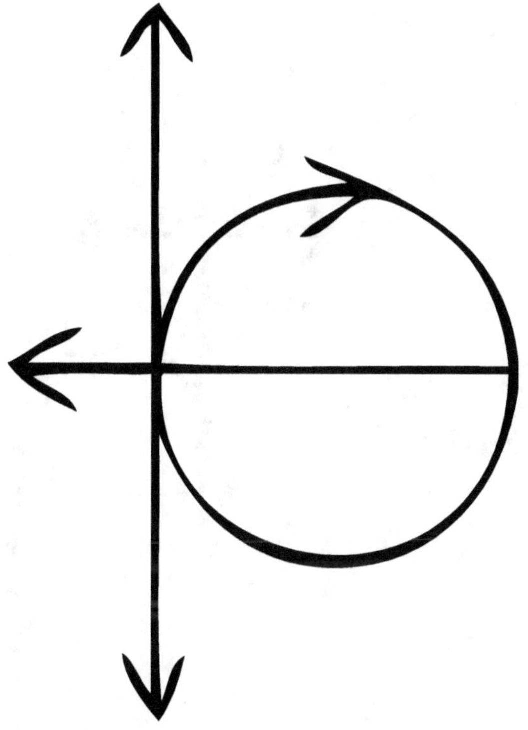

FREE WILL AND FREEDOM OF CHOICE

Fourth Seal

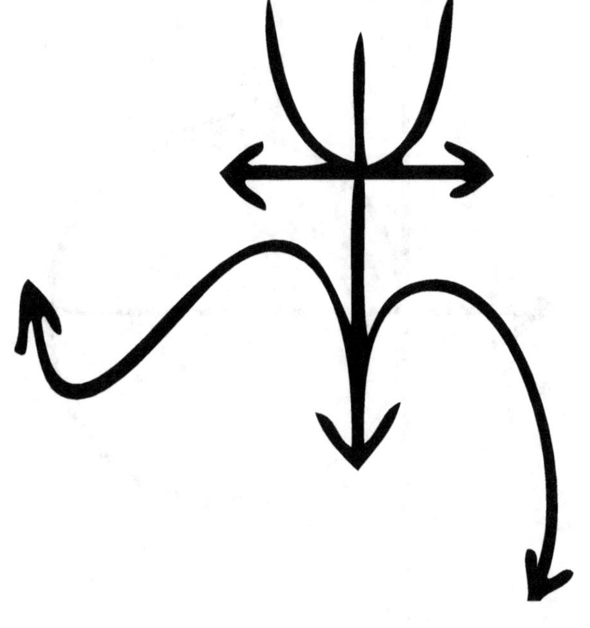

Know Thyself

Fifth Seal

Value and Trust

Sixth Seal

Act with Consciousness

SEVENTH SEAL

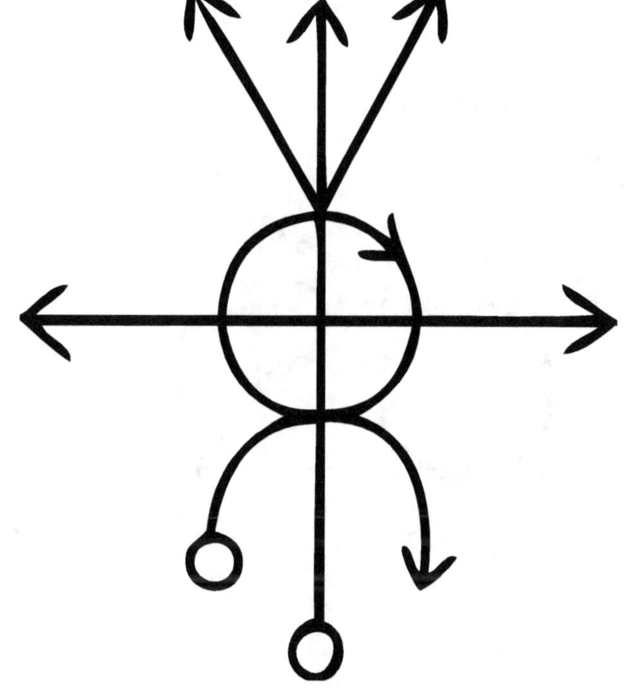

MEDITATE AND CONVERSE

Eight Seal

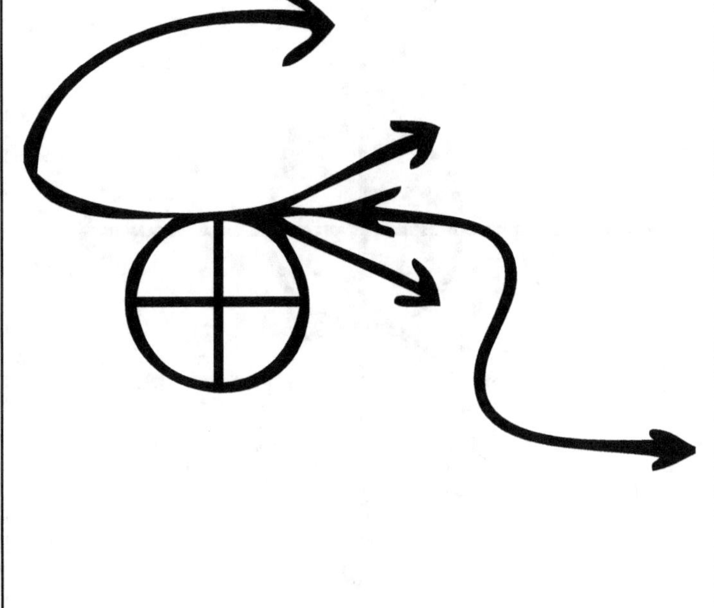

Invoke Often

Ninth Seal

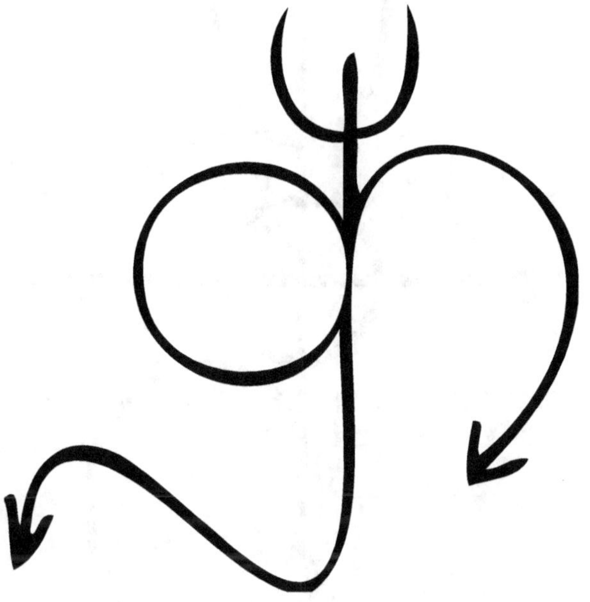

The Science of Goodness

Tenth Seal

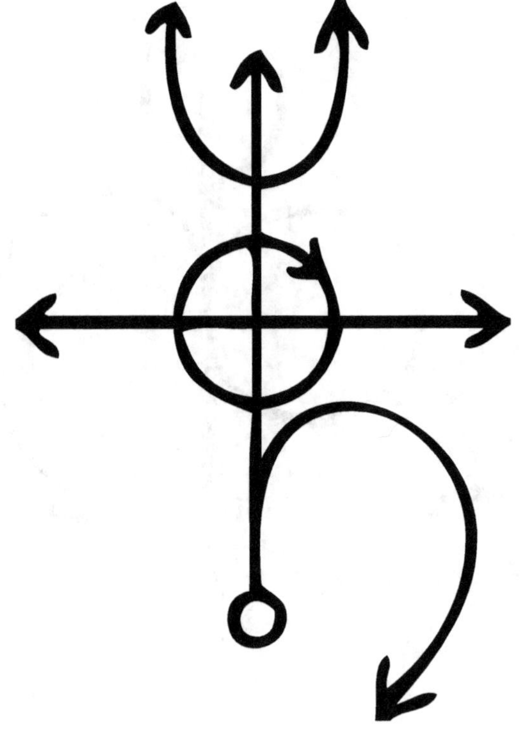

Mastering Draconia

ELEVENTH SEAL

PRESERVING AND TEACHING DRACONIA

Conclusion

I HOPE with all my heart that you will appreciate these new practices of Draconic Magick as much as I have had to receive, practice and transcribe them here to your attention. True, it took me a long time before I could give you this second tome. It wasn't my intention to make you wait so long! I dare to believe, and hope in my heart, that the wait was well worth it and that this book will find a tiny special place in your occult library.

Magick Science is so large and vast that any magician will always find the tools necessary to perfect his magickal and draconic practices. Sometimes it is enough to listen, to look a little further over the horizon, to follow our inner Being and of course... our fellow dragons and faithful familiars, given their race or the kingdom they inhabit.

Here you are, a few more pages have been added to the great book of Draconic Magick. Much re-mains unknown. Draconia is full of surprises and it is up to us, practitioners of the Magickal Arts, to find the hidden paths leading to the coveted treasures of knowledge and eternal wisdom.

Until the next opportunity, dear friend daraco, I greet you with the Triple Sign...

Appendix

I n order to provide as much material as possible so that the exercises contained in this book can be practiced without having to refer frequently to the first book on Draconic Magick, I offer as a complement the two essentials mentioned here and there throughout this book. The reader will find the full unabridged version of the Major Rite of the Draconic Cross as well as all the explanations relating to visualization in *Draconia*. He can therefore read it if he wishes in order to obtain more information and perfect his learning.

THE TRIPLE SIGN

The Triple Sign is a very noble magickal gesture that is given solemnly, with dignity and respect. This is a special ritual greeting. It is thus given with the right hand which remains open, fingers joined together:

- Touch your forehead with your right hand.
- Then touch your heart (or lips).
- Then, finally, open the arm slowly outward, palm up.

I have noticed over the years that the practice of the Triple Sign was unconsciously done by myself in a slightly different way. I have never discussed this variation, as it is quite suitable, if not better. My personal way of doing it is as follows:

- Touch your forehead with your right hand.
- Then touch your lips.
- Then touch your heart.
- Then open the arm slowly outward.

There are two reasons for giving the Triple Sign:

Greetings:

When you need to greet dragons or any other Entity in a dignified and respectful manner, then you can make this gesture. It will tell them that their presence is welcome.

Closure and Banishings:

This method is most commonly used. The magician gives the Triple Sign following an invocation, an important statement, to mark the end of a special stage during a ritual (as an ecclesiastical would do with the sign of the cross) or to conclude a ceremony. When used in this way, this sign symbolizes that you are taking a significant pause, a conclusion, a banishing of energies or a silent way of saying *so mote it be*.

The Draconic Cross

- *Part One: The Draconic Cross*

Touch your forehead and vibrate: **ZAH**
Point down and vibrate: **ONDOH**
Touch your right shoulder and vibrate: **MIH**
Touch your left shoulder and vibrate: **BUZD**
Then join hands and vibrate: **PAID, STELOI**

- *Part Two: The Formulation of the Pentagrams*

Trace the Pentagram in the East. Vibrate:
ORO-IBAH-AOZPI
Trace the Pentagram in the South. Vibrate:
OIP-TEAA-PDOKE
Trace the Pentagram in the West. Vibrate:
MPH-ARSL-GAIOL
Trace the Pentagram in the North. Vibrate:
MOR-DIAL-HKTGA

- *Part Three: The Evocation of Draconic Kings*

Open your arms, forming a cross, and say:

Before me stands SAIRYS
Behind me stands NAËLYAN
To my right stands FAFNYR
To my left stands GRAËL
For about me flames the Draconic Pentagram,
And within me shines the Six-rayed Star.

- *Part Four: The Draconic Cross*

Touch your forehead and vibrate: **ZAH**
Point down and vibrate: **ONDOH**
Touch your right shoulder and vibrate: **MIH**
Touch your left shoulder and vibrate: **BUZD**
Then join hands and vibrate: **PAID, STELOI**

9 782898 062971